How To Get
Black on Track

A SELF-EMPOWERMENT GUIDE

FOR PEOPLE WHO ARE READY
TO MAKE A CHANGE IN THEIR LIVES
BY STARTING WITHIN *"SELF"*

ALICE T. CROWE

Eye of Atum Press • *Nyack* • *New York*

1914-358-7617

How To Get Black On Track!

Library of Congress Cataloging in Publication Data

CIP   ISBN

94-090916   0-9645984-1-8

Crowe, Alice T.

How To Get Black On Track

The subject matter that this book contains is in no way intended to be legal, medical or financial advice. If expert assistance or counseling is needed, the services of a competent professional should be sought.

Dedication

To all wise elders who feel useless as they are nearing the end of their journey in life and whose trains are awaiting that final stop to join the ancestors...

To all Black youth who feel that they are on a train going nowhere without a purpose, without direction, and with nothing to live for...

I write this book in effort to bring the passengers on these two trains running in opposite directions back on track so one day they meet at the same station, at the same time.

Finally, I write this book for people who are ready to make a difference in their lives by starting within self.

Acknowledgments

In preparation of this manuscript the author is indebted to many people and sources of information. The many valuable suggestions and conversations, criticisms are likewise appreciated.

A special thanks to Mr. *Charles E. Crowe* for his patience and editing of this book. Thank you to all of the loyal supporters of Zola Gallery.

To Gwendolyn and Charles Crowe for giving me the stick to beat back with! (Mom & Dad)

To Alicia (Sis) for editing and being my best critic

To CURTIS for your support, understanding, and technology!

To Big mama for giving me a cable chord to the source

To Andre & Dave for the use of the office for the 1st draft

To Bro. Warren for telling me to stay and fight!

To the late Carl Ferguson for exposing me to media

To WLIB-AM & the ICBC family for being my home based university

To Kim, Marie, Lashaun, Michael, Arshene, Antonio, Geramiah & Michelle for your loyalty at Zola Gallery

To Aakif for the enlightening conversations

To Listervelt Middleton and *For The People* for being the source for my home University

To Dr. Edmonds for teaching the truth at the University

Mamadi Nysuma for T.R.U.T.H.

Thank You!

This book is written in the spirit of "Nia" Purpose.

AUTHOR'S REQUEST

Please pass this book around. Give one as a gift to a friend, loved one, family member, a stranger, or some one in need of getting on track.

Preserve and protect Black scholarship and research. *At the end of this book is a list of resources, and institutions to support.*

How To Get Black On Track

$10   Mail order add $2

Shipping and   Handling

plus .75 each   additional   book

Write: **EYE OF ATUM PRESS**
P.O. Box 88
Nyack, NY 10960

v

"Education is the medium by which a people are prepared for the creation of their own particular civilization, and the advancement and glory of their own race."

- Marcus Mosiah Garvey

"Real education means to inspire people to live more abundantly, to learn to begin with life as they find it and make it better..."

- Carter G. Woodson

TABLE OF CONTENTS

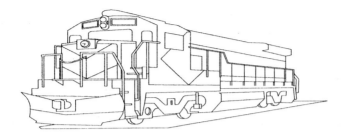

INTRODUCTION

⌘

THE NIA FORCE: Our Train; Symbol; Concept
        "Go free or die..."   *- Harriet Tubman*

    You are about to begin a journey in which you will take your mind on an exodus. The goal of this trip is truth, action and self-empowerment. The train you will board is the *Nia Force*. *"Nia in Swahili means purpose."* The purpose of this journey is self-improvement.

    The *Nia force* is not a real train ride but an idea that will take you to your destination. Your boarding pass is your desire to make a change in your life. It does not matter what your position in life is -- it is never too late to turn your life around. You can be in a good job wanting more independence. You can be in a bad relationship or good one. You can be recovering from substance dependence, or religious overdose. You can be a student enrolled in school, or in need of education or training. Yes. You can change.

3

How To Get Black On Track!

It is never too late to get Black on track as long as there is tomorrow. The location of the platform for this train ride is wherever you are standing. The time of departure is now!

*M*ake certain you tell no one of your journey, where you are going, or if you will return. When you do you scatter your energies and forces out there will stop you, attempt to sidetrack you or prevent you from getting on track. You must go alone and travel light. Go and tell no one is the plan. That means tell no one of what you desire to do in life.

*T*he baggage you will leave behind is negative thinking, complacency and mental bondage. The *Nia Force* is neither an express nor a local train, but a redemption train that allows one a second chance to go into the right direction in life. It is to be hoped after reading and following the suggestions in this book you will become the conductor of this *train*. You will learn to think and follow your own mind.

*T*his book has five chapters. We will journey to each one by our imaginary train the *Nia Force*. On our first stop we will *Follow the North Star* to take passengers on the road to self discovery. It is here where you might be reacquainted with yourself and discover your hidden genius. You will learn how to set realistic goals and fulfill action plans to achieve those goals and start a *Revolution* within.

*A*s we venture onward the Nia Force will make a second stop to allow you to *Get Your Ticket to Ride*. You will learn the *science of mind power* and the art of *believing* in yourself. You will learn how to avoid becoming s*idetracked* by others.

4

The third stop will be an open invitation for all passengers to *Come Aboard the Nia Force*. As a passenger you will find the *Keys to Understanding* what hinders Black achievement. You will also visit the *Underground Railroad* to gain a historical outlook on the idea of liberation.

On our next stop, *Watch The Closing Doors as the Nia Force* travels to the year *2000*. You will attain insight into the future to develop a program in preparation today. The Nia Force will take a short cut to the *Information Superhighway* to take a look into *Cyberspace*.

The final *Destination is Non-Stop To Excellence*. You will visit the learning center, the **Sankofa Shule**. Here you will learn how to establish home based learning centers, study groups, or community educational programs. *Sankofa* is an **Akhan** proverb that *means to go back to fetch what was lost*. You will learn the important lessons in history to better your life and your community today. The *Nia Force* will make a few of pit stops to make certain its passengers are okay.

All aboard the *Nia Force*! Last call to get on board! The *Nia Force* has a non-stop destination to success. Do not miss the call to get on board! The train is going to go forward. There is no turning back. You have three choices. You can watch it pass, stand in its way, or get on board.

Remember, do not look back unless you want to go that way!

"Even if you are on the right track, you will be run over if you just sit there." *Will Rogers*

5

Chapter 1
FOLLOW THE NORTH STAR!

(ST-5) *Keep on moving forward! Don't look back unless you want to go that way.*

1

THE REVOLUTION BEGINS WITH SELF!

Attack the enemy within and the enemy outside you can not harm you...

Change your attitude and you will change your life...

Before healing others, heal thyself - Wolof Proverb

At the end of each year most of us engage in a popular and familiar annual ritual. We gleefully sip champagne momentarily leaving behind last years broken promises, good times, or misfortunes. This ritual is known as the *"New Year Resolution"* routine. We promise ourselves, our friends and loved ones we will not let another year pass in our present condition. This year we are really going to change.

Our promises seem impossible to keep, yet we repeatedly say "Never again!..." With a toast to the new year we blow our noise makers, scream "Happy New Year," and tell our new pact to everyone. The hours between December 31 and January 1st seem like an eternity. We can't wait to meet our challenge.

We believe when the clock strikes 12:00 a.m. January 1st something magical will happen. One minute passed midnight we will automatically, stop overeating, start exercising, or flee from a miserable relationship. We will find a better job, stop eating red meat, stop smoking, or keep any other promise. Most of us start the first week in January with good intentions. We are determined not to let any of our friends or families take us off our new program. That is, if we created a new program.

We soon find out it takes more than just a personal promise to get rid of the negatives in our lives. Our commitments fade in a flash. We are back to business as usual. What happened to our new year vows? If we even made any, they are all on hold until next year. Does this sound familiar? *The New You Revolution* can begin at anytime. It does not call for the clock to strike midnight to kick off a grand ceremony. You do not need to toast champagne. It does not matter how many times you fall off track or become sidetracked, the revolution within is always possible and timely.

Are you happy with your life? Are you satisfied with your progress in life? Maybe it is time for a change. It is probably time for a *New You Revolution*. What is a *New You Revolution*? It is a change in the way that you think. Most people go around in life believing that all they have to do is change everything around them and their lives will change.

We think that if we change other people or work toward turning around events that make us feel powerless we will find happiness or success. Nothing could be farther from the truth. If you would like to change anything in life, first you must begin with that which you have control and the power to change. You have the ultimate power to change yourself. All of the other things, people, events may never change. They have no real impact over your circumstance if you change.

For example, if you are in a miserable relationship where the other person has one too many character flaws you will soon find out that they may never change. The only thing that you have the power to do is change how you will react to that person or decide whether you can live with their flaws. You may never make them change their habits.

If you are in a bad job situation and you think that you can change your coworkers, supervisor, or customers, think again. You can change your attitude and decide that you will not permit others to upset you or control your emotions.

Changing your life is like planning a trip: *You have to find out where you are now, decide where you would like to go, then figure out how to get there from where you are.*

THE THIRD RAIL

Make that change...

Brothers and sisters get ready for a rough train ride ahead. Make certain you are sitting down and you place your feet firmly on the ground. You are venturing into the zone of danger. Be forewarned, on account of there may be a few losses. The risky fate that requires caution is the revolution "of self." The revolution "of self" will never be televised!

The fleeting revolution is a radical shift of events in your life. It is very difficult for many people to envision themselves making a complete turn around of their life or even a partial improvement. This is because one's sense of inner blindness often curbs one from honestly looking inward and seeing the weak areas that need improvement. This inner blindness is a lack of consciousness.

Those weak areas are often our real enemies in life. They live deep within us all and are our beliefs and our attitudes. Beliefs and attitudes are not only hard to change but often hard to find. We do not understand why events in our lives seem to stay the same. Seldom do we ever expect to analyze this antagonist. The enemy within is a parasite that destroys lives if left undiscovered. The best remedy to conquer the enemy within is to annihilate it by exposing it. This will raise our level of awareness.

The revolution or change must come from deep within our beings or we will never see any real change in our lives. It is a mistake to think a change in our physical appearance, our hairstyles, our names, our rhetoric, our diet, our religion, or our actions will be sufficient to cause change in our lives. We have only touched the surface of the enemy's camp and if anything we will only reap temporary positive results.

Unless we change the channel to our mental programming and change our way of thinking, we will only be going through the motions. We will be fooling ourselves and other shallow people into thinking we have control over our lives. We will have only discovered a false sense of true awareness without really finding our hidden inner power.

Your beliefs control your actions. If you are a negative apathetic person and you have a cynical reaction to everything positive, the world will treat you in the same negative manner. Nothing positive can ever happen for you as long as you are thinking negatively and go around throughout life with little consciousness of your negative attitude. If you would like to attract a positive situation, compatible relationship, etc., you must first be positive. You must be the type of person you are desiring to attract.

Are you an optimistic person or are you highly critical? Do you have a positive mental attitude and do you feel you can achieve in life? Do you ask yourself *"Why bother?"* Do you make excuses that change is too hard or it's a waste of time? What you believe is what you can achieve! What do you believe?

ON THE ROAD TO SELF-DISCOVERY
IN SEARCH OF SELF

Who are you? Do you know? Who are your friends and associates? Do they define who you are? Have you lost touch with yourself? Do you take time to listen to yourself? Go back and look through your old things like old photos, papers, awards, letters this will help you to get in touch with your old self. Take a minute to reflect on these items. Revisit a time when you felt the most productive and successful in your life.

We all have about three to five talents or abilities we do not know we have. However, many people leave their abilities untapped and unfortunately take their talents and gifts with them to their grave. All types of talented people fill the cemeteries; the *also rans; runner ups; and wanna bee's.*

Where are all the profits of these talented people? Who has reaped the plums of their efforts? What happened to all the potential cures for sickle cell disease, cancer, prize winning novels, consciousness raising rap songs, economic blue prints for the Black community, contributions to history? All of these possible contributions died too and we buried them 6 feet underground. The living were never able to share in these talents.

The non-living never made their special donation to life, never made it to the finals. These gifted individuals are no longer among the living. Nature relieved them of their responsibility to improve the quality of society. What is your excuse? Are you using your talents and abilities?

What makes people tap into their inner selves and discover their hidden talent? Is there some trick or secret to finding our own special talents? No. There is no trick or secret. People discover their hidden talents in many ways. Some people follow their own minds and listen to what their inner voices tell them to do. Others overcome obstacles, and tragedies that force their hidden talents out of them.

To find that hidden talent you have inside, you must first do some inward reflecting and critical analysis. Ask yourself these questions. *Are you happy with your life? What have you contributed to life? What are you capable of contributing? What is the value of your human capital? What area(s) in your life can you improve?*

Begin your journey into self discovery by writing your own eulogy

If you were asked to speak at your own funeral what would you say about yourself? How would you like the world to remember you? Refrain from saying you were friendly, successful or religious. If there is something in your life that you had the power to change what would it be? What type of person were you? How have you contributed to the betterment of your community?

If you have a special talent, mention it in your eulogy. If there was something that you wanted to do for someone else what was it? What expression best describes you? Were you a member of any organizations? What were your hobbies? What did you leave behind? Complete this exercise in your personal journal, or answer the questions mentally.

Compose a personal speech

If you had to make a speech to a large audience what would you say? *Last speech by ... Message to whom?* What would you say and to who if it were your last words? What about your physical appearance. Did you look your best at all times? Were you earning a living by doing something that you enjoy? How did you treat your friends and family?

Stand up in front of a mirror, make eye contact and speak. Tell everyone all the things you want them to know? Don't hold back! Now analyze your speech. *Was this a quick speech? Was it boring and uninteresting? What can you do to change? What steps can you take to make that change in your life? Do it now!*

13

THE NEW YOU REVOLUTION

Develop a *New You Revolution* routine. Never start your *New You Revolution* by partying or abusing addictive substances. Make a list of improvement areas and work on one area daily for a week. Oversee your progress in your personal journal. Use the above two exercises as a personal assessment and develop your own self-improvement plan. The *New You Revolution* can begin today. Listen to self-improvement tapes daily and get rid of loud music and pointless hours of television from your routine.

AREA	*ACTIVITY*
Employment	*Work diligently/Job search*
Health	*Exercise /Diet*
Education	*Read/Research/Library*
Spiritual	*Meditate/Prayer,* *Libation/Nguzo, Saba, Ritual/Worship*
Self-esteem	*Personal grooming/ Colon care*
Creative	*Sing/Dance/Art/Music/Writing*

➤*Exercise* - The best way to break out of a rut or slump is to exercise. It gets the blood flowing and energy moving.

➤*Order* - Clean up your surroundings and organize your things. Develop a daily routine and try to get up an hour earlier each morning.

➤*Relax* - Relax and concentrate on reducing nervous tension and anxiety. You can accomplish more in a relaxed state of mind. Use motivational or self improvement tapes daily.

(Les Brown -- Live Your Dreams) (Baruti Kafele -- Goal Setting A Black View) (Dennis Waitley -- Psychology of Winning) (Zig Ziglar -- Goals) (Brian Tracey -- The Psychology of Achievement)

The 7 principles of Kwanzaa* are positive words to use daily

"Umoja (Unity) To strive for and maintain unity in the family, community, nation and race."

"Kujichagulia (Self-determination) To define ourselves, name ourselves, create for ourselves and speak for ourselves instead of being defined, named, created for and spoken for by others."

"Ujima (Collective Work and Responsibility) To build and maintain our community together and make our sister's and brother's problems our problems and to solve them together."

"Ujamaa (Cooperative Economics) To build and maintain our own stores, shops and other businesses and to profit from them together."

"Nia (Purpose) To make our collective vocation the building and developing our community in order to restore our people to their traditional greatness."

Dr. Maulana Karenga founder of Kwanzaa

15

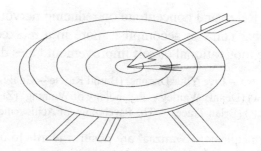

SELF-IMPROVEMENT HINTS

✔ Dress and look your best at all times

✔ Improve your personal grooming/hygiene

✔ Practice good manners & etiquette (change rude behavior)

✔ Exercise - improve personal appearance

✔ Open up your mind. Visit museums, cultural events

✔ Spend time thinking

✔ Change your diet- visit a health food store

✔ Health - Get a medical exam, counseling, support group. Improve your diet.

✔ Job skills - training program, continuing education

✔ Expand your vocabulary. Invest in vocabulary builder tapes or books

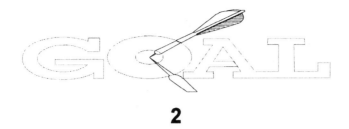

2

GOAL SETTING

Seriousness of Purpose

A man who won't die for something is not fit to live

- Martin Luther King

*To find your **purpose**, you must search yourself and with knowledge of what is good and what is bad, select your course, steering towards the particular object of your dream or desire.* - Marcus Garvey

Little by little the bird makes its nest - Haitian Proverb

As you journey toward self-awareness you will discover that you have hidden strengths and talents. When you set goals in life fulfilling them will not be easy. The major thing that separates a high achiever from a low achiever is goals. What are goals? Goals are things we wish to achieve in life. They are our ideas, dreams or aspirations.

The key for tomorrow is what we do today. It is never too late to set and achieve goals as long as there is tomorrow. It does not matter how old you are or how long you have been sitting out on the side lines of life. You can always

17

accomplish what you set out to do. Yes you can w*rite your book - own your own home - get a better job -get your driver's license, make a music recording and more.* Goals are always attainable as long as they are within reason.

What makes a goal achievable is that it is in reach. Our goals must make us stretch and grow. If we find ourselves bending over backwards to get our goals then we need to reevaluate our goals and perhaps set new realistic ones. Remember, when the road in life is too easy get off it because you aren't going anywhere. Life's roads have bumps, potholes and road blocks. There is an unwritten law that states "*You can not get something for nothing.*" There is always a price to pay for everything one gets in life. In other words, there is no such thing as easy street.

Generally, it takes obstacles and setbacks for us to realize what our strengths and powers really are. These obstacles are often stepping stones when we look at them in another way. The puddles in our paths that force us to take detours are actually the force that leads us into self discovery and personal power.

Obstacles are really nothing more than difficult choices we should make. These choices are cleverly disguised as problems. Make that difficult choice or decision and stand by it. Overcoming obstacles build strength and courage. There is an age old expression that says, "*If it doesn't kill you it will make you stronger.*"

Stop riding aimlessly on someone else's train and get on board your own train, (the *Nia force*). Develop a seriousness of purpose plan for your life.

✋ PERSONAL INVENTORY

Ask yourself some critical questions. Be honest with yourself!

1. Are you happy with your life? (job, career, home, relationship, physical appearance)

2. Do you have an agenda in life you can clearly articulate?

3. Do you have clearly defined goals in life?

4. Are you an independent thinker or do you allow your friends or loved ones to dictate your point of view?

5. Are you reactionary or proactive?

6. Do you spend quiet time thinking about what you want to do in life?

7. Do you allow your friends to occupy most of your free time?

8. Do you talk more than listen?

9. Do you make excuses for failure?

10. Do you experience anxiety when you are faced with change?

19

GOAL SETTING

Everyone must move through life with a purpose or a vision. Goals are in essence dreams realized. If we do not have any dreams or desires in life, we will go through life winging it from day to day getting caught up in things we had no intentions of doing. We become floaters drifting around wherever life takes us.

There are *three* types of goals in life, *Short-term goals, Mid-term goals* and *Long-term goals. Short-term goals* are immediate, *Mid-term goals* are the bridges you use to get across to accomplish your long-term goals, and *Long-term goals* are for the near future.

Besides goals there are personal victories that are the minor accomplishments that lead to bigger achievements. Personal victories give us mental comfort and self confidence. They also raise our *I can do it* attitude.

GOAL SETTING EXERCISES

1. *Write down in your goal journal the following categories:*

Work/Career/Job

Money/Health

Life Style/Possessions

Relationships/Spiritual

Creative self-expression

Fun/Travel

Personal growth/education

Think about your present life situation and write next to each category some things you would like to do, change or improve in the future. Write what ever comes into your mind. Keep your list simple. Then next to your list write *WHY* you wish to have these things. This will help you determine if you really want the goals you have chosen. Be honest with yourself. Write those things you want for yourself and not what you think other people expect out of you.

If you are in a slump or **RUT**, set a goal to wake up early in the morning. Get out of the house, walk, or do something other than sleep and watch television. If you have been sitting down all week, or month, your energy level might be low. You need to get things moving. Exercise will get your blood flowing and help you develop a routine for action and self-discipline.

<u>EXERCISE</u>: Select one activity and stick to it. If it is weight lifting, do it on a regular schedule. Jog or walk regularly -- first thing in the morning.

Make a personal promise to yourself to get up just one hour earlier for one day and then try it for a week. This minor first step will be the action needed to achieve bigger goals. Always reward yourself when you accomplish a small personal victory. Do something nice for yourself.

2. *Write down in your goal journal: My Five Year Goals.*

Describe fully where and what you would like to be doing in the next five years. Write down things that are meaningful to you. Do not worry about your age or present situation. Remember be honest with yourself. No one has to see your list but you.

3. *Write in your goal journal:* ***My One Year Goals:***

Will these goals get you to your five year goals? For example if your five year goal is to own your own home then your one year goal should be to save money. Now write your six month goals, then one week goal. Reduce your goal list to three or four things. Be realistic about how much you can actually accomplish in six months, a week, or day. For your daily routine make a **To-Do-List.**

4. *Sit quietly and visualize your goals.* Develop mental pictures of your ideal scene in life. Cross off some of the goals you have achieved on your list. Make new ones! Remember to celebrate your goal achievement by doing something special for yourself. Do not be discouraged if you do not achieve all the things on your list. Are goals permanent? Are they etched in stone? Of course not! Feel free to change them as often as necessary.

NOTE: Choose one major goal that requires most of your attention. Choose minor goals that won't sidetrack you from your major goal. It is sometimes hard to achieve a number of big goals at the same time. Have patience. Our big goals require more of our time, focus and energy.

GOAL SETTING TIPS

✍Get a personal planner, organizer or calendar and decide to take control of each minute of your life. One can not be truly successful without a well thought out plan. We must write things down. It is okay to test our memories often but we show real commitment to that which we wish to achieve by writing down our goals.

✐Get a daily planner or keep a journal. Write down your goals and put date next to them of when you would like to achieve them. Combine your goal list into your daily schedule. Is the date that you choose etched in stone? Again, of course not! Often things don't go on schedule. The dates are only a suggested timetable. Write down your short term goals or things you wish to achieve in the next week.

4 STEPS TO GOAL ACHIEVEMENT

*W*ritten. Until you write goals down, they don't have any power. Once you commit goals to paper, they become a reference point something concrete that can be a constant reminder of what you want to achieve. The act of expressing your goals tangibly in writing gives them the power of your conviction.

*P*lanned out. Develop a strategy for achieving your main objectives. Then put together an overall plan that includes the most essential steps for achieving the goal. Large or long-term goals should break down into smaller short-term goals. Assign a time for each short-term goal. Identify resources that can help you achieve your goals. Anticipate possible obstacles and develop a plan for dealing with them.

*M*onitored. Review your goals periodically. When the results fall short of your goal, identify any problem areas and take corrective action. If your actions are working, keep on doing the same things. If they aren't working, then try something else. You will have more opportunity to gauge your progress when you monitor goals daily or weekly. Frequent monitoring keeps you on track.

*P*ersistence. Never quit or give up on your goals. Make adjustments if you have to or change your approach or direction. All your goals should be achievable, but they should make you stretch. As you accomplish more and more goals, you will experience success after success, and accomplishment will become a habit.

GOAL SETTING SUMMARY

✒ *Make a list and identify the things you would like to do.*

✒ *Set a deadline next to each goal.*

✒ *Determine what are the obstacles to achieving your goals.*

✒ *Identify the people and or groups, organizations that you need to work with.*

✒ *What steps must you take to achieve your goals?*

Answer the following questions about Goal Setting

What skills or knowledge are necessary for your goals?
What are the rewards for achieving your goals?
Are the goals that you have chosen worth having?
What is the price that you are willing to pay if you do not chase your goals?
Are you willing to pay the price?
Reward yourself after you achieve your goals

✍ The trick to goal achievement is to discover the talents that you possess and put them to use. Try to achieve little goals or personal victories so that you advance to more challenging goals.

✍ Visualize, or see yourself doing those ideas on your goal chart. With any goal or plan you must do homework or research.

✍ Have you fallen into a slump? Look up and regain your balance! Be tough on yourself and life will be easier on you. There are a lot of people who can stop you temporarily, but only you can stop you permanently.

PERSONAL CHARTER *a writing given as evidence of a contract or plan - - a grant of power.*

A *Personnel Charter* is a creed that we follow strictly without deviation. It is our own program that we have dedicated ourselves to sticking to until we achieve our goals. After we reach our desired goal we make new charters and continue the process.

The *Personal Charter* should begin with a mission statement. Take about 15 minutes to think about your statement. Then write your mission statement in your personal journal.

A Mission Statement

☞ *To educate and uplift myself mentally and spiritually so I will be able to build and better myself, my family and community. I will read.*

⇟ *I will give up tobacco & alcohol and I will refrain from staying out after hours.* I will be gainfully employed and actively seek a job or get training so I will be competitive by the year 2000.

⇟ *I will* **BUY BLACK** *and support Black institutions. I will work to reconstruct Black Civilization.*

A mission statement is an affirmation of our purpose in life. Write your mission statement affirmatively and never conditionally, e.g., *only if, unless.* Write it with command language such as *I will*, or *must* never, *I may* or *I hope*.

Every day that we rise, we should reaffirm our purpose. Write out your mission statement and place it in a highly visible place so that you can see it daily. *It is through our purpose that we develop our vision by seeing our purpose in action.*

Our mission statement is our personal promise that we make to ourselves. It is a vow that we take promising ourselves that we won't fail. We communicate to our inner voice that we will win by any necessary means.

Devise a Road Map so that you can lay the tracks into the direction of goal achievement. Sketch pictures of goals, ideas, aspirations in the order in which you wish to attain them. Next draw lines connecting each goal so it looks like a map. Hang this picture on your wall so you can visualize. Visualization is key to getting what you want!

PERSONAL JOURNAL

I would like to encourage you to get started now on your own process of self-realization and growth toward self-improvement. A good way to begin is by starting a personal journal. You do not have to spend much money on one. Get a notebook for jotting down notes, ideas, goals, etc.

✐ This journal is just a log book for how things are going in your life as you pursue your mission of getting Black on Track. Write down your goals and set a time and date you want to achieve them. Your personal journal is your record of your self-improvement.

✐ Each time you get an idea, dream or unique thought write it in your log. If you are feeling anxiety or powerlessness, write it! If you have a particular problem then, write it! Each time you achieve a goal cross it off the list. Make a symbol next to the goals that are still incomplete. This will remind you know that you still have work to finish.

✐ By keeping a personal journal you will be able to keep a record of your progress and gauge if you are staying focused. Write the date next to each time you complete a goal. Keep a record of your thoughts daily or often. Write in a narrative form as if you are talking to another person. Be as brief as possible but descriptive. Always take time out to read your journal.

27

A sample page of your journal might look like this:

MY NEW YOU REVOLUTJON Log

Date 4-3-94   Time 6:00 p.m.

Goals:

1. Get More exercise. Lose 10 lbs.   8-1-94

2. Read More books   4-3-94

3. Get a better job   12-1-95

4. Continue My education   5-1-94

Action Plan:

1. Get up an hour early and do yoga exercise

2. Go to the local library and get a library card.

3. Draft a resume/ call contacts

4. Take computer classes at the Computer Center/ Call today

Attitudes: I'm feeling very positive about my job interview in two weeks . I am a little nervous about taking a computer class. I have been out of school for 15 years.

Obstacles: I may not have enough background or training for that new job.

Ideas: I will take out books, video or audio tapes on bookkeeping so that I will be prepared to answer any difficult questions on my job interview.

Notes: I got a library card, took out a great book and a home study course on bookkeeping. I found out about two more job opportunities from the library bulletin board. I'm sure glad I read that bulletin board at the library.

An example of an Action Plan

My New You Revolution - Goals

1 GED

2 Job Skills

3 Housing

4 Bank Savings

ACTION PLAN Goal #1 - *GED*

Step 1 - Go to local library get library card. Research *GED* programs, get review materials, exam date.(Use action plan for other types of exams).

Step 2 - Study Schedule

Step 3 - Practice exam taking at least two weeks before the exam.

ACTION PLAN Goal #2 - *Job Skills*

Step 1 - Evaluate your present skills and abilities. Research specific target areas where jobs should be available such as in *sales, cooking, security, driving, computers*, etc. If you are in a profession that is having a slow down in hiring, research possible hot areas where companies might be hiring.

Step 2 - Go to local library read the daily newspaper and check the library bulletin board for help wanted information. Research free training programs.

Step 3 - Make a list of personal contacts and leads for job information. Draft a resume or work history outline.

Step 4 - Go for it!

ACTION PLAN Goal #3 - *Housing*

Step 1 - Evaluate your finances. Check the local library or community center bulletin board for rooms to share or apartments. Contact your local YMCA or YWCA. Call a local real estate company to view local housing in the area that you wish to live.

Step 2- Contact the sources.

ACTION PLAN Goal #4 - *Bank Savings*

Step 1- Go to the local library and inquire about local credit unions in your community. Ask friends or neighbors where they bank. If you need information on budgeting and finance check your local library for video or audio taped home study programs. Write *In the Black Productions* Inc. P.O. Box 1229, New York, NY 10185.

Step 2 - Open up a savings account. Plan a weekly budget to deposit money into your account on a consistent basis.

* Research retirement plans, investments, pensions and other business opportunities.

GET ORGANIZED

"Order, a place for everything and everything in its place."

Organize and plan your life just as you would plan a party, meeting, wedding, etc. Step by step patiently logging ideas. Invest in a daily calendar or a hand held electronic schedule organizer. Many of us seldom, if ever log our ideas. As a result too often we are latecomers or we just plain miss out on great things.

Plot your course with a blueprint. Manage your life. Develop a daily schedule and analyze how much sleep you are getting. Early to bed early to rise! The secret to getting Black on track is to get organized. Too often we underestimate the zero percent organization in our lives as evidenced by the mounds of dirty clothing, disheveled important papers and list of phone calls to return.

Do you spend endless hours watching television, socializing with friends every weekend for the past five years? Are your investments in beer, potato chips, movies, dance steps, videos, and rallies? Have your hobbies caused a lack of productiveness and success in your life?

If you answered yes to any of these questions then, you may suffer from the inability to draw the line when necessary. You may lack focus, or strategies and tactics to achieve your goals?

Can we ever correct our errors now that they have become embedded in our daily routine? Yes! The redemption train does come your way when you are truly ready to make a change in your life.

DEVELOP THE MASTER PLAN

Your new journey into self-discovery has begun and now you must properly lay down the tracks to reach your destination. Make certain that all of your tracks are going into the right direction. The imaginary tracks that you put into place are blueprints for achieving your realistic goals.

A train will derail or go off track if the train is moving too fast or if we improperly lay the tracks. You too will you go astray in life or become derailed if you do not properly plan or anticipate possible conflicts that can cause you to detour. Planning is key to your survival. Failure to plan is planning for failure!

We often face sudden factors that disable us. At times even the best thought out situation can become destabilized. What should you do when caught off guard? Use what you have until you get where you want! Help will always come from the least expected source.

Get into shape spiritually, physically and culturally. Become aware of the details of your life. A *plan* is simply what you aim to do, and how you aim to do it.

THE PLAN: Develop a *Master Schedule, Master Daily Plan* and a *To-Do-List*.

The **Master schedule** divides a year into 4 or 3 month blocks. When we approach a year in 4 month blocks, e.g. January - April, May - August, September - December, we simplify our strategy. This makes goal planning easy. Every 4 months we can evaluate our progress. Let's look at an example. Our goal is to save money in one year. We must first determine how much money. Let's say we want to save *$3000.* We must then divide that by *12* months which is $250. We can now plan to save *$1000* every four months.

By breaking our year into months we become more aware of the time limits to our goal. If we wait and see how much we can save at the end of the year we might be like most people. We will wait until the last month of the year and try to save all that we can. At the outset saving for a year seems simpler if we do in four month sections.

MASTER SCHEDULE PLAN

JANUARY - APRIL   *save $1000*

MAY - AUGUST   *save $1000*

SEPTEMBER - DECEMBER   *save $1000*

OR

JANUARY - MARCH   *save $750*

APRIL - JUNE   *save $750*

JULY - SEPTEMBER   *save $750*

OCTOBER - DECEMBER   *save $750*

---

*The **Master Daily Plan*** is a schedule of each daily activity to accomplish your goal. Before you can make a master schedule you must first determine your daily schedule and how many hours and what days you will work toward your goal. Let's assume that our goal is to pass an exam. The exam date is April 2. We would use the schedule below from January until April.

MASTER <u>DAILY</u> PLAN

Daily Plan **Mon. - Wed. - Fri.**

6:00 A.M.   RISE   EXERCISE

6:30 A.M.   BREAKFAST

7:00 A.M. 8:00 A.M.   BUSINESS   MATTERS

9:00 A.M.-5-P.M.   WORK

6- P.M. - 7 P.M.   DINNER

8- P.M.   STUDY FOR EXAM

9-P.M.   FREE TIME

10-P.M. SLEEP (OR) 11- P.M.   SLEEP

The **_To-Do-List_** is a list of the important matters that need your attention. It is a daily reminder of what you need to do today. Each time you complete an item on the list cross it out or put a check next to it. Make your _To-Do-List_ at night for the next day or early in the morning. A _To-Do-List_ is a blueprint for your daily routine.

To-Do-List - 10-12-94

1. Pay Bills

2. Go to the Supermarket ✓

3. Return important phone calls

4. Doctors appointment ✓

5. Research business opportunities at the library

POINTS TO REMEMBER

✍ Start your day on the right track by getting up extra early in the morning.

✍ Organize your day by making a _To-Do-List_. If you are a morning person then do the most important things on your list first thing in the morning. Plan your week in advance.

✍ Develop a strategy for completing your list. Plan to attack each day as if it were your last. Always begin each day with action.

HELPFUL HINTS

- *Get a calendar and plan your daily routine for the entire month.*

- *Keep all important phone numbers in the same place -- get an organizer or planner.*

- *Keep all appointments in a calendar.*

- *Write down all of your projects. Make categories for your things. Develop a filing system for your important papers. Clean and organize your closets.*

- *Develop a weekend schedule for working on your special projects. Modify your schedule accordingly if you are off on weekdays.*

- *Make a schedule and stick to it for a day, a week then a month. Remember, do not allow others to distract you while on schedule unless it is an emergency. Set some firm rules.*

- *Go to a local library if disturbances at home distract you. At the end of the day write how you are doing in your progress journal.*

* For information on books to help you get organized see the resources section at the end of this book.

✋ A PITSTOP FOR PERSONAL INVENTORY

From time to time throughout this journey it is necessary to make a short stop to see if the passengers are doing okay. We are taking a pause to get you to take stock. There is no need for alarm this is just a check up to help you stay on track.

Spend a little time now answering the questions below. Remember, be honest with yourself, and let the answers to these questions guide your next steps in this journey.

● Have you read the previous chapters carefully including the introduction?

● Do you understand the true meaning of the *Nia Force*?

● Have you done the exercises and answered the questions in the chapters?

● Have you set realistic goals?

● Have you visualized your goals?

● Have you identified your strengths and weaknesses?

● Are you rewarding yourself for your achievements no matter how minor?

3

SURVIVAL TOOLS

Reality hits hard and sometimes TKOs

Only the assertive and aware can counter the blows...

Strategy is better than strength - Hausa Legend

"Never let the left hand know what the right hand is doing..."

Our journey in life will be turbulent. The path we choose will have puddles and obstacles. One thing is certain; obstacles are unavoidable. Always remember, if the road in life is too easy get off because it is going nowhere. As we pursue life's daily course, we will face surprises and setbacks. People will deliberately place obstacles in our path because they do not want us to succeed. Other obstacles will be lessons that life is trying to teach us.

While venturing off into this mysterious trip called life no one ever really gives us specific details or warning about which type of barriers we might meet. We soon discover we will surely need *Survival Tools* to take with us on our journey through life. What are *Survival Tools*? *Survival Tools* are affirmations, daily meditations, biblical warnings, African proverbs that we reflect upon to get strength, protection, and guidance when we set out to do a task in life.

People will pick up different *Survival Tools* depending upon the tracks and directions they travel. Along each pit stop in life we find new *Survival Tools*. We can never abandon our old tools because we never know when we might need to use them again. We must always use the same *Survival Tools* if we get positive results the first time.

Survival Tools are also survival strategies used during slavery. Plain and simple they are lessons from our elders and other wise people of victory in difficult times.

Survival Tools are tactics that we use to help us secure goals and protect us against life's lessons. A chef would not attempt to cook a meal without the proper utensils or recipe. A mechanic would not attempt to fix a car without the proper tools. You should not venture into life without some type of survival tool or strategy that helps you reach your desired result.

Given that obstacles are really choices that we must make, *Survival Tools* help us make those choices wisely. The *Survival Tool* that is recommended for this journey is,

Never let the left hand know what the right hand is doing...

This is an age old survival strategy used by Africans for many years. Simply put, it is the art of deceit and fooling your enemies by keeping them in the dark about your true objective in life. In other words, it is keeping your mouth shut and using your silence as your best weapon.

This tactic is no doubt very important because it requires that you keep quiet to everyone about your plans in life. This includes relatives, loved ones and close friends. If others ask "What are you up to these days?" Simply answer "Just keeping busy." You must resist the urge to brag about your goals.

Only share that which you desire to do in life with resource people or mentors who can help you realize your goals. Otherwise, do not let the left hand know what the right hand is doing by keeping totally silent.

How does this idea work? You do understand that it is rare the right hand does anything the left hand is unaware. Think about it! How do you keep the left hand from knowing what the right hand is doing? You create a very clever and convincing sham with your left hand. Now do you follow?

You will learn more by listening than talking. You might be saying to yourself "deceit is lying." When you do not openly confess to the world everything you aim to do in life you protect your self from the unknown.

By keeping your plans to yourself you will prevent outside forces who aim to circumvent you from succeeding against you. Historically, the art of deceit has been a clever strategy for African survival. It appears that the Africans trust was often betrayed by folk with less than good intentions. When we blabber mouth our plans we give others a clue to what we want in life and we help them stop us.

Lesson #1   Every smiling face is not there to help you!

Lesson #2   Believe in yourself and you won't be easily deceived.

Lesson #3   The buzzards are always waiting to do a clean up job on those forms of life that give up the struggle.

Lesson #4   Turn around is fair play!

Lesson #5   Hold on!

Lesson #6   Nobody tells all he knows.   - *Senegal*

During slavery, slaves used deceit as a tactic to escape the plantation. Harriet Tubman used deceit to make at least 19 journeys to freedom. According to Molefi Assante, during slavery our fathers and mothers perfected their predictions of white behavior. They began to tell only what was acceptable and thus concealed their true beliefs, impressions, and ideas behind masks. It was better, in a survival sense, to tell whites what they wanted to hear and continue to live than to tell unpleasant facts and be sold down the river.

We live in a society where divide and conquer has been the most successful tactic to curb Black progress. This has made it difficult to trust everyone. That is precisely why "deceit" is a crucial tactic. Slavery has created a community of turncoats, Nat tattlers, sellouts and apologists. Some Black folk may not be willful loyalists of an imaginary "*Master*," but unfortunately the condition of dependency upon others for survival makes this statement true.

You must have a game plan when you are practicing deceit. Keep in mind that when you pretend you must not do so for the sake of amusing. That is wasteful energy. You will attain absolutely nothing. You must always pretend with a goal in mind.

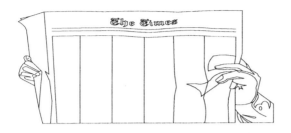

Does the world views you as, unable to think or function? You can fool your doubters by deceiving them. When your skeptics fail to firmly focus on you and they count you out as a contender in life, you can excel without their distraction.

When Harriet Tubman was close to becoming captured by a nearby bounty hunter who she thought recognized her, she pretended to read a newspaper. She prayed she did not have it upside down when he spotted her. Everyone knew that she could not read. She successfully fooled her captors with deception.

"Warfare is the art of deceit, therefore when able, seem unable; when ready, seem unready; when nearby, seem far away; and when far away, seem near ...Attack (the enemy) where he is not prepared; go by way of places where it would never occur to him you would go."

* The Art of War, Sun TZU.

Chapter 2

GET YOUR TICKET TO RIDE!

(ST-7) *Keep your eyes on the light and you won't see the dark side*

4

OPEN UP YOUR MINDS EYE!
The Science Of Mind Power

Put your mind to it... Free your mind...

What you think makes you what you are...

The spirit never sleeps, it guides us in many ways to do the limits, unknown, impossible and helps us perform miracles...

It has often been stated that we are the output of exactly what we think. Our minds give us the capacity to think. It is our mind or what we think that make us what we are. What you believe your self to be is what you will become.

If you believe your self to be bad, undeserving, a loser, then that is exactly what you will become. If you believe that you are talented, good, a winner then you will become all of those things. Why is this notion correct? Because, along with beliefs follows action.

Our behavior is grounded upon what we think. If we believe we are not free and our happiness, liberation and future well being depend upon another, we will act as if we are dependent and incapable of thinking for ourselves. We will act like a child living in *'daddy's'* house unable to make our own decisions in life.

Our actions will soon conform to our thoughts. Our thoughts are molded and manipulated by outside forces such as television, radio, newspapers, media, and daily interaction with people. Often times if these forces have a negative aim they will influence us by weakening our self confidence or break our spirit. We quickly lose our ability to concentrate on anything positive about ourselves.

Mind control is extremely effective in manipulating behavior. That is why advertising is so effective. Billions of dollars are spent annually by corporations to conform the publics' behavior to buy products by putting ideas into consumers minds. We are told which toothpaste will make us happy, or which toilet paper will make our families more unified. We are reminded daily that the type of car we drive tells the world who we really are.

There are numerous theories about the mind, it's power and the subconscious. The subconscious mind is also known as the spirit. The spirit is the basis which gives meaning to life. According to Iyanla Vanzant,

> "*Spirituality is a journey inward that connects you to the pulse of the universe as it is expressed through your being...*"

Success and self-empowerment are a state of mind. To feel empowered or powerful you must first believe that you are. A state of mind does not require anything other than the proper mental attitude. Your mind is like a computer. If it is turned on it can become useful. If motivated and given the correct program, goals and plans your mind can enable you to accomplish all types of desired results.

Remember, the revolution begins within. By opening your minds eye you can look within to offer solutions to whatever problem you face. When we operate our lives with the aid of the spirit, the precise tracks will automatically fall into place as if a magic hand has laid them.

Your subconscious mind is your source of power. It is the act of believing that gets the power started. Why is it so important to focus on mind power? There is a battle being waged for our minds. A basketball player first mentally visualizes the ball going into the basket before he takes a foul shot. He sometimes pretends to take the foul shot before the referee hands him the ball. A figure skater visualizes a skating routine before getting onto the ice. He/she never sees him/herself falling.

See yourself accomplishing goals, getting out of a slump, operating your business. See yourself happy in a wonderful relationship, financially secure or owning your own home. Envision being the kind of person that you would like in your life. Visualize the thing first in your mind's eye and your behavior will conform to your thoughts.

We can take back control over our mind by opening up our mind's eye and focusing on our agenda. There is a biblical warning that is also a *Survival Tool, "Where there is no vision the people perish."* Without a mental picture one can not accomplish very much. Visualize your ideal scene in life and then conform your behavior to your thoughts. If you truly deserve that which you desire, it will be yours.

Close your mind to negative thinking. Counteract negativity with positive thoughts. Become a great doer in

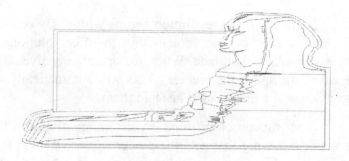

action. Listen for the sound of the train while you are sleeping. Answers, ideas, solutions to problems may come to you as a dream. Our subconscious mind always talks to us.

Keep paper and a pen near your bedside so you can write down what comes to mind in the middle of the night. Do not try to interpret your dreams right away. Just focus on the images and the sounds you might hear. You will see the importance of the vision much later. The importance of the vision may come to you a week later. Your dream might just be a solution to a problem you are having. Remember, do not tell anyone about your vision or you will lose the connection with your subconscious mind.

Is there any evidence the mind is a miraculous power? You may dream about someone you have not spoken with in months. Suddenly, that person gives you a telephone call or you accidentally meet them in the street. You might have a problem and no idea who can help you solve it. A stranger approaches you out of the blue and offers you a solution to that problem. Do these scenes sound familiar to you? Your mind is an awesome power. Use it!

5

YOU'VE GOT TO BELIEVE IN YOURSELF!

Yes You Can!

If you have no confidence in self you are twice defeated in the race of life. With confidence you have won even before you have started. - Marcus Garvey

Believe in yourself when you have no one else to believe in...

As you continue your journey on the Nia Force, be forewarned you might come across more difficulties. These barriers will prevent goal achievement. There will be events that will make you want to get off the train before you reach your destination. The rough rides ahead may be discouraging. You may cast doubt on whether you can make it another foot. *Faith* makes all things seem possible. Belief in yourself and your abilities will help you get passed problem areas.

Simply saying to ourselves yes I can, or I can do it is not enough. It goes deeper than that. *Faith* is an inner feeling that we truly believe that we can. It is trust and confidence in ourselves. *Faith* is the ability to dig down deep inside ourselves and find that hidden energy that will enable us to not only climb up the rough side of a mountain, but if necessary to move it out of our way. *Faith* means a firm

49

belief in a higher power. Believe in yourself and a higher power will guide you in the right direction.

IMANI - FAITH

Faith ✝ Discipline = POWER!

Empty prayers ✝ Inaction = NOTHING!

At different times of the day our conscious speaks and tells us what we really need to hear but we are resistant and we turn a deaf ear. When we listen to our inner voice we are thinking for ourselves and not following behind others. If we always look for a leader to follow we are following his thoughts and he or she will lead us anywhere that his/her mind goes.

Listen to your mind. Think and speak for yourself then you will not have to worry about any one paying off your leader to suppress your community. We must believe that the goals, dreams, or aspirations we choose are possible. We must visualize doing, being, or having what we desire in life. We must develop strong belief systems in ourselves and know for certain we will not let ourselves down or even fumble. This belief system must be coupled with discipline and action or else we are doomed for failure.

Hoping and praying are worthless without action. We have never gotten anywhere by just hoping and praying. Our history has shown if we believe in an idea strong enough and apply the key action we will pull through in difficult times.

Never allow anyone or anything to break your spirit and beat you down. Our African spirit is what we firmly embraced as our anchor in life to survive slavery. We lost our homeland, our mothers, our fathers, our religion, our culture, our family, our language, yet we somehow managed to maintain a firm death grip on our spirit.

It is through the African spirit that we are able to survive slavery with sanity and free from the type of vengeance that other groups hold who have suffered atrocities. The African spirit is the only thing that enables Black people to; still laugh, sing, dance, build and work hard in life.

Individuals have the power to achieve against all odds. The spirit of one being can have a tremendous impact on an entire nation. Think about Harriet Tubman and her spirit to free countless slaves from bondage. Read the biographies of Dr. Martin Luther King, Malcolm X, Marcus Garvey, Denmark Vessey, Nat Turner, Sojourner Truth, Rosa Parks, Mary McCloud Bethune, and others.

Faith only says that things are possible. It does not guarantee certainty in results. If there is a possibility then there is a chance. A mere chance is all that one needs in life to make things possible. Believe it is done and it shall be done.

"When a needle falls into a deep well, many people will look into the well but few will be ready to go down after it." - *Guinea*

"If you are building a house and a nail breaks, do you stop building, or do you change the nail?

-Rwanda - Burundi

"A wise man who knows proverbs, reconciles difficulties." - *Yoruba*

6

DON'T GET SIDETRACKED!

Each generation must out of relative obscurity, discover its mission, fulfill it, or betray it   - Franz Fanon

Do not allow others to take you off your track. There will be jealous people disguised as friends and supporters who are really confidence shakers and detractors. You take your focus off your goals and dreams when you allow envious people to fool and sidetrack you.

Resentful people will try to engage you in pity parties. They bring you their miserable problems because they recognize your growth, change, and strong spirit. These are the people whose behavior identifies them more precisely than their names. The folk who have little confidence in you or themselves are, *Doubters* and *Deniers*, *Do nothings*, *Disorganizers*, and *Coat-Tailers*. These folk would like nothing else than to see everyone around them fail.

Doubters and *Deniers* are people who spend their days criticizing and complaining about their lives. They are always available to give you a reason not to try. They will put their arms around you when you fail not with the intent to comfort you or make you stronger, but to hold you back from your goals. They pretend to be your best friend so they can get close enough to you to knock you down. Watch out!

53

Then there are the *Do Nothings*. These jealous people are always available to talk about problems over which they have no control. They spend their days watching soap operas, mindless TV talk shows, or reading mud slinging tabloids that defame celebrities, movie stars and other successful people. They call you up daily to keep your mind focused on unimportant things. They have no goals of their own because they spend most of their time sitting out on the sidelines of life gossiping about people who are achieving their goals.

When we become knowledgeable about who we are we walk with confidence and direction. This is obvious even to a stranger. Once you develop your plan and agenda stick to it. Be forewarned, there will be people boarding your train who will attempt to sabotage you.

The people who will undermine you are, S*alt Sprinklers*, because they are always quick to put salt into someone's game. These folk are hard to recognize at first. They may be members of your own family, close friends or people you have never seen before. They will come as friends who aim to help you or disguised as references ready to misguide you down a dead end track. Be able to see through these fakers by sticking to your own plan and conducting your own train. You might have to avoid these people for a while.

Staying focused means setting boundaries with people and keeping them from controlling or over influencing your life. Likewise, there will be people who will want to take up your time with unproductive time consuming political meetings. Be very polite yet inform these detractors that you are working on a number of projects that require a lot of time and attention. Tell them that if something opens up you will call them. Tell them Bye-Bye!

When you gain recognition as a goal achiever people will flock towards you to better their own position. These people are called the *Coat-Tailers*. The Coat-Tailers are wanna bee's who want the world to know they have celebrity friends. Ignore these status seekers. Shake your *coat-tail* regularly and whatever is clinging to it will fall off.

Do not allow anyone to tell you that you are not capable of doing that which you desire. Don't take no for an answer! Surround yourself with positive people. Positive people are people who have goals. They spend time thinking of solutions to problems. They are *solutionaries* not *reactionaries*. They bring hope, optimism and energy to others. They are creative, confident and always seeking to better themselves. Find a mentor or someone who can guide you in the right direction.

We can get easily distracted by friends, family and others who take up most of our time with their problems. Remember, you must not allow your train to stop before it reaches its destination. Keep focused on your agenda!

REBEL FOR HIRE!

I once met a young college student who was what I like to call a *rebel for hire*. He took on all the political problems on his college campus. He was at every rally and lecture. He read every book he considered politically correct. He wore all the popular political medallions and T-shirts. He studied the *struggle* with a passion and could copy talk the rhetoric of the most dynamic radical speakers.

55

The College overlooked his financial aid application the next semester. He was forced to leave school. He rebelled for every cause but his own. He was sidetracked by *the struggle* and has yet to understand that the goal was to get the skills in order to make a difference. Without an education, he was totally useless to *the struggle*. All he could possibly be was another addition to the powerless fist shakers, moving mouths and raising attitudes.

If your agenda is to get an education, stay in school. Make a commitment to stick to your agenda and take an oath to finish what you start.

✋ PITSTOP FOR PERSONAL INVENTORY

It is time for another pause to see how the passengers on this journey are doing. We have covered some very rough roads and you might be a little rattled. Remember answer the following questions as honestly as possible.

● Are you keeping silent about your true plans and goals?

● Have you picked up any *Survival Tools* on this trip?

● Have you worked toward your *Goals*?

● Are you rewarding yourself for your achievements no matter how small?

● Have you been writing in your *Personal Journal*?

Chapter 3

COME ABOARD THE NIA FORCE!

(ST-9) *Take a journey in your mind and exit onto the platform of reality.*

"Proverbs are the daughters of experience"

-Sierra Leone

"Only when you have crossed the river, can you say the crocodile has a lump on his snout"

- Ashanti

"It is the calm and silent water that drowns a man"   *- Ashanti*

7

THE KEYS TO UNDERSTANDING

The creation of a nation begins in the homes of its people...

Find a place for yourself in this world in this lifetime among your people...

The journey through life is like a train ride. Birth is the boarding pass to begin this trip. Historically the symbol of a journey has been used to describe our plight, and our struggles. We will journey by train because it is strong, momentous and stops for no one. No human being can out run a train that operates at maximum efficiency.

The main focus of this imaginary train ride is the experience that takes place between birth and death. This is the most important part called life; and by far the most complex. Once one enters the platform called life there is no turning back. The interesting thing about this journey is that we never know where it will take us but we are certain that one day it will end when we reach that final stop.

Life teaches us lessons by placing stumbling blocks and hurdles in front of our paths. On this trip called life we are driven down dead end roads. We have set backs and disasters that frustrate us and make us want to give up on our goals and dreams.

How To Get Black On Track!

We carry excess baggage filled of burdens that weight us down and break our spirit. We track along in life unhappy as difficulty after difficulty greet us along the way. The power we thought we once had to direct our imaginary trains into the direction we want them to go has disappeared. We soon discover we are on the wrong track or otherwise going nowhere in life.

Did you know the tracks for your life have already been laid for you? Tracks are guide posts or directions in life. All you have to do is find the right tracks for your journey in life, stay on them, and follow them to the end.

This guide is a handbook for holding on when the ride is long. There are numerous reasons why we may find ourselves in unwanted circumstances. Our train maybe going out of control, moving too slowly, or it is temporarily out of service.

What do we do when we do not like where we are stationed in life? What do we do when we feel our lives are boring or we can not seem to get out of a slump? Do we give up and except our situation as permanent? Should we feel sorry for ourselves and make excuses for why we can not achieve what we desire in life? Of course not!

We must immediately stop the train that is taking us in the wrong direction. Get off at the next stop and if you start walking help will always meet you half way. Define your new direction. Do your best to get back on track if you have fallen off track. Then do what ever is needed to become successful and accomplish your goals.

Remember, your post in life is never permanent. The close encounters, the unhappy job situation, miserable relationship, lack of education and training, substance addiction, hard times, whatever the situation, is only a pit stop in the journey of life and will pass only if you allow it to pass.

The key to getting past a rugged trip is to hold on to your grip. When you find the correct track on which to ride you must do so with the zeal of a locomotive. When you feel that you can not go on in life because life has beaten you down, hold on tightly because a redemption train just might be coming your way. *Always keep the faith!*

Whenever you feel weak and weary like a train, draw your energy together and push onward. Your train will overcome obstacles just by determination, persistent action and faith. Get a dream, or set a goal today that takes you off your slow track. Get a system of organization that will make your train run on schedule and stop that runaway train that is out of control. Make that crucial choice and solve that problem or overcome that obstacle holding you back.

If you are one of the many sleeping giants, awaken quickly and board the train to get Black on track. There is no time to waste you must get moving into the right direction now. Come aboard the train to help empower yourself and build your community now. If you think you have missed the train before move quickly there is no time to waste. You may be able to catch the train at the next stop.

BREAK THE CHAINS & FREE YOUR MIND!

Untangle the mental web

Freedom comes from understanding who you are...

When you feel good about yourself you find it easy to join in with others. You are more likely to think creatively and act upon your goals and desires in life. Life gets rough and you get tougher. Life knocks you down but you get back up with ease. It is your attitude and how you feel about yourself that will determine how far you will go in life.

Self esteem is a growing steady course that is never stable. There are many people with high self-esteem who do not always feel happy, enthusiastic, comfortable, confident or secure. There are times when these people feel fearful, sad, unfit or unworthy.

The difference between a person with high self-esteem and a person with low self-esteem is that the former is able to accept the unwanted feelings they have and still know they are basically okay people. People with high self-esteem gain their source of approval from within and not from outside sources. According to George Subira, author and business educator,

> *Deep down in the consciousness of many Black folk there are many feelings of insecurity, doubt inferiority and confusion relative the their ability to function within the broader White world.*

These feelings of insecurity and doubt prevent us from reaching our true potential in life. They are responsible for making us fall off track or lose sight of our goals in life.

It is extremely difficult for Black people to understand which track they are on in life. How can we be clear about what we can become in life, when we are confused about who we are? Moreover, George Subira states,

> *"The most fundamental aspect of racism the Black American experiences is that they are held out to be different and inferior to the rest of the people we refer to as Americans."*

If a person is shown negative images on a consistent basis, told they are nothing and have contributed nothing to society, ultimately that person will experience low self-esteem. What can we people do to feel confident and self assured? One key to turning around the dynamic of "inferiority" is to understand its source and do away with it. Simply put, we must get rid of the *"Badge of Inferiority"* by refusing to wear it. And how can we get rid of something that has been deep-seated in our minds for almost four hundred years?

We can start by learning the truth about our experience in the world. We can define and understand what our role is in restoring ourselves back to our traditional greatness. It is not enough to just learn who is who in Black America in February. We should go farther back to the source - the primary source is Africa.

Besides positive self talk we can also undo the negative myths that perpetuate inferiority complexes. We can replace negative reinforcement with positive reinforcement. We can start believing in ourselves.

How To Get Black On Track!

It is regrettable but true that most people have been miseducated about the Black experience. The education system, media and religious institutions continuously spread myths and false information of history that is nothing more than Eurocentric ethnic cheerleading.

Consequently, some people believe the lowly plight of Black people is permanent and ordained by some higher force. We are taught that Black history begins and ends with slavery and we have no homeland to return to either physically or mentally. According to Carter G. Woodson,

> *"The educational process inspires and stimulates the oppressor with the thought that he is everything and has accomplished everything worthwhile, depresses and crushes at the same time the spark of genius in the Negro by making him feel that his race does not amount to much and never will measure up to the standards of other people."*

The reason why some Blacks are inactive is because they lack understanding of who they are. Some have in essence fallen off track, lost their ability to be independent, take initiative, and control in their lives.

According to Dr. Asa Hilliard, historian, psychologist, people of African descent suffer from a mental condition called *"Conceptual Incarceration."* This mental condition affects the thinking process of millions of people of African descent. Moreover, Dr. Hilliard states that people of African descent are victims of fabricated histories. They are often confused, isolated and disoriented as a result of a loss of historical continuity. The remedy for this mental condition requires that the victim make a unilateral mental declaration of independence. It is Dr. Hilliards contention that,

> *"Free and critical minds can emerge only by a return to the source -- the primary source. A free and critical mind takes nothing for granted and is not intimidated by "authorities" who frequently may be more confused than the general public. Free and critical minds seek truth without chauvinism and shame."*

Many survivors of slavery uphold a permanent servile demeanor in life although the physical aspect of slavery no longer exists. Carter G. Woodson states:

> *"When you control a man's thinking you do not have to worry about his actions. You do not have to tell him to stand here or go yonder. He will find his "proper place" and will stay in it. You do not need to send him to the back door, he will cut one for his special benefit. His education makes it necessary."*

To remedy this harsh reality and better our lives we can take a fresh approach and get Black on track by engaging in a self-help program that includes goal setting, agenda building, African history and re-education for self awareness.

When one is Black on track he/she identifies with an African consciousness and mode of intelligence. And he/she understands fully his/her contribution to the world. This new found relationship with Africa and a unilateral declaration of independence from Europe, is essential to regenerate a new desire to build and dream.

Slavery, and the massive attempts to strip away the rich heritage, institutions and culture of Black people have left many of us without an identity and in disarray. We have the difficult task of repairing the tremendous damage.

Frederick Douglass once stated that "*power concedes nothing, it never has and it never will.*" We can not expect other cultures who oppress us to help us get out of our condition. Of course there is a very real oppressor that is dominant in our lives daily which is the system of racism. However, this is no excuse for giving up on life and feeling overwhelmed and hopeless. Moreover, it is no excuse to treat ill feelings and depression with chemicals. According to Dr. Frances Cress Welsing we must understand the dynamic of white supremacy and counter it. We must not fear it, continue to deny that it exists or allow it to hold us back.

We can promote community learning and literacy by creating study centers in every home by the year 2000. We can also build institutions and enterprises in our community so that we will survive the future challenges and become a viable force politically, economically, globally and spiritually. If we fail to take heed to the warning to *Get Black on Track* we will not survive the future.

The next major area that Black people can focus on is economics. If we failed to include economics as an issue in the Black community our strive for freedom, and human rights would be incomplete. Don't shop where you can't work! Stop financing your own oppression. Buy Black. The idea of buying Black is a viable solution to many of the problems that plague the Black community. We can support our enterprises and strive to maintain them so that the Black community is gainfully employed.

According to George Subira, Black folk should pursue the field of sales. The first reason why we need to learn the new skill of selling is because many of our old skills are of no economical use anymore. We can not make it off minimum wage jobs any more.

In the midst of all the chaos and confusion surrounding the plight of Black people, unity and self-help is one answer. Self-help has been the agenda that immigrant groups have used to advance in society. Blacks in America must look toward each other for the answers and solutions to problems. Collectively, Blacks earn more than 460 billion dollars a year. If we funnel a quarter of this total back into Black enterprises, we would strengthen the Black position and be less dependent upon the government and others for our existence.

In addition, Black Americans spend approximately $12.9 billion on clothing each year, $450 million on potato chips. How many potato chip companies are Black owned and operated? How many manufactures and distribute their garments? Some of the most influential highly educated, high profile Black Americans spend $3 billion dollars a year on conventions, and seminars. This is a sad commentary when we understand that there is not one major Black owned hotel.

Black spending habits must change. When we decide to patronize groceries, clothing stores, lawyers, doctors, auto dealers that are not Black-owned and Black- operated there is a loss of about 1 million jobs. This results in the prevention of the formation of Black capital.

How To Get Black On Track!

Blacks must show group unity on all levels. We must support Black owned businesses and business owners must seek to do business with each other. Through the disciplined practice of unity we can better our position in society. We have tried everything else and have failed. Group unity has worked success for other immigrant groups. Although Black people are not immigrants nevertheless Black people and immigrants share the bottom position in the socioeconomic structure of America.

We can define our stake in the future and determine that we will survive and achieve. We must know who we are and fully understand *our past*. One who learns from the past seldom makes similar mistakes in the future. The study of the past should not be for the purpose ethnic cheerleading but to extract the necessary *Survival Tools* to excel in the future.

We can win the battle being waged for our minds if we focus on our own excellence. This does not require that we become apologists, engage in tolerance training, or teach other cultures to love us. *Anti-bias, Multi-culturalism, Inclusion, Tolerance, Cultural Diversity* are all diversions from the important issues that the Black community must focus upon. There will be significant changes in the year 2000. We can adapt our thinking and behavior to accommodate these changes.

Lastly, we must improve ourselves as individuals. We must commit to a self-improvement program that will enable us to make the necessary revolution within.

68

8

THE UNDERGROUND RAILROAD

"I nebber run my train off de track and I nebber los a passenger"

- Harriet Tubman

The next stop on this journey is a visit to the Underground Railroad. The *Underground Railroad* is a unique historical symbol of freedom. In 1845 the *Underground Railroad* was the source that enabled many Africans to flee from bondage under the harsh and brutal system of slavery in America.

Although it was not a real train nor was it underground it was nevertheless a network of anti-slavery activists who helped *slaves* escape captors to freedom in the North to Canada. The *Underground Railroad* also enabled *slaves* to flee south to Florida. Blacks fought a dragging battle for sixty years in America's southern-most region, Florida without the assistance, funds, or advice of northern whites.

The Fugitive Slave Law of 1850 made it extremely unsafe for *slaves* to remain in the North. This law established the legal right of recovery of run-away slaves where ever found in the United States. Often *slave* masters would give a general description of a *Black* person and anyone found who remotely fit the description was returned back into slavery without any defense. The new bill forced marshals of free states to hunt down fugitives within their borders and return them to their masters.

Slave owners were desperate to contain the *Negro*. A *Negro* did not have any right to a trial by jury and could not testify in his own defense. A commissioner who ruled in a fugitive case would earn double the fee if he ruled in a slave owners favor. The severity of the fugitive slave law created an overwhelming atmosphere of fear. Many sympathizers were too afraid to assist runaway *slaves*.

Years later the Supreme Court, in a five to four decision held in the *Dred Scott* case that, under the Constitution even a free Negro who had formerly been a slave had no rights that the white man was bound to respect.

Harriet Tubman bravely challenged this law. She was the clever and cunning conductor of the *Underground Railroad.* She was well known as the Moses of her people because she made 19 or more journeys from the southern slave plantations, taking *slaves* as her passengers up north to the free states and Canada.

Harriet Tubman was born into slavery around 1820 in a town called Bucktown near Cambridge on the Eastern Shore of Maryland. (There is doubt as to the exact birth date of Harriet Tubman.) She was born Harriet Ross and was one of eleven children. She ran away from slavery at the age of 25 and by 1852 she was a legend.

In the 1860's with rewards topping almost $50,000 Harriet Tubman pressed on deceiving bounty hunters. She successfully completed every journey guided by the *North Star*.

The *Underground Railroad* was an idea that symbolized a mass exodus to freedom. The train idea is vital to Black people today because it can be used to free our minds. The physical aspect of slavery is over, yet locked in our brains are the mental conditions of slavery.

The purpose of studying the *Underground Railroad*, or any historical event for that matter, is not merely to raise self-esteem, or prove to whites that we are worthy of equality. We should not learn about our story to teach the world that we have a glorious past. Our studies should be to acquire knowledge of survival tactics and strategies that are useful in our battles today.

What we must extract from the teachings of Harriet Tubman is that she had a mission to set her people free. She had a *goal* that she worked diligently toward achieving daily. Although times were hard she did not stop striving nor did she allow anything to break her spirit. She would never be reduced to a *slave* in her mind.

Harriet Tubman found her true purpose in life. Freedom was an idea that she unequivocally embraced -- and without it, she was prepared to die. Her words emphasize her sentiments as she often stated, *I started with the idea in my head, there's two things I've got a right to, death or liberty.* With the magnitude of an army and the spirit of the almighty inside her she made an impact on the face of the universe.

How To Get Black On Track!

The Moses of her people achieved her tough mission to let her people go often at gun point giving her passengers no other choice but death. She often stated "Be Free or Die" to *slaves* who were uncertain about fleeing.

Harriet Tubman was a cunning and cautious conductor. She searched the faces of her passengers for possible spies or turncoats as she warned "dead men tell no secrets." She set her family free and was able to liberate approximately 300 others. On her last journey in 1857 she rescued her parents and carried them to Auburn New York.

Of course, she prayed and asked for divine guidance to assist her in her mission to free her people. Harriet Tubman was in fact a truly spiritually based individual; still she did not rely solely upon prayer to achieve her objectives in the *Underground Railroad*. She had a strategy and a plan of action that she used in her 19 or more journeys from plantation to plantation.

The North Star was a symbol that had a tangible explanation to its followers and believers. It was a landmark in the journey toward freedom and liberation. It symbolized time, direction, and reassurance from a higher force of the righteousness and victory of the struggle to be free. Yes, Harriet Tubman sang *Swing Lo Sweet Chariot*; Go Down Moses, and about going to the *Promised Land*.

Harriet Tubman sang these familiar words:

"I'm sorry I'm going to leave you, Farewell, oh farewell, But I'll meet you in the morning, farewell, oh farewell.

I'll meet you in the morning, I'm bound for the
Promised Land, On the other side of Jordan,
Bound for the Promised Land.

I'll meet you in the morning, safe in the
Promised Land, on the other side of Jordan,
Bound for the Promised Land."

To some people who heard her sing these words in the middle of the night, she was a god sick irritant needing a good whacking to quiet her. To others who heard these words she was a liberator scheming to lead her people to freedom.

In many of her songs she referenced heaven. She sang so many spirituals that people often associated them with her. Many folks believed that she wrote them herself. These expressions had tangible meanings of very real places. She used these spirituals as her coded message to communicate to *slaves* her action plan for their immediate liberation.

Harriet Tubman understood the science of mind power. She followed her thoughts that led her to free her people. The train is not just a symbol but a powerful idea if used properly. The improper use of empty symbols and ideas have been detrimental and costly to Black people for generations. Too often we get lost in the symbolism or the mysticism of an idea and seldom are we ever able to gain focus long enough to achieve any significant results.

Moreover, when we are successful in our undertakings we are seldom able to reapply the idea to achieve the same successful result twice.

For some of us, our religious beliefs have contributed to our embracing of ideas and images that we improperly apply in our lives daily. In other words, we pray for what we want, pray to rid a bad situation and hope to get our desired result. We are also taught to believe that some mystical icon will surface and make everything better in our lives.

Unfortunately, wishing won't bring results. We all can agree wishing gets one nowhere because there is no such thing as a magic genie who will pop out of a lamp and grant us our desires. When we apply a little discipline, action and logical translations to the symbolism in religious myths, we can achieve our goals with our own efforts instead of just endlessly waiting on another source to produce results in an after life.

The train is significant because it symbolizes motion, strength and persistence. These are characteristics that Black people must adopt along with discipline and action. A train has an agenda and only rides in the direction of its tracks. If the train is derailed it gets back on track and ventures on its course. Like the train we too can create an agenda of our own that guides us in the direction that we choose instead of blindly following the course of others.

Our train, The Nia Force is rapidly approaching and those who are ready will get on board. Those who are not ready will get left behind. We do not have time to wait for people who are not ready. We do not have time to apologize to people who feel offended by our desire to be independent.

We are on a mission and our destination is non-stop to excellence. We do not have time to continue to teach other cultures all about our humanity. We do not have time to include ourselves in discussions led by others on what we should be doing collectively. This train is going to go forward. There is no turning back.

Our liberation depends upon whether we can listen to our own voices, think, act, speak and represent ourselves. We are on an imaginary train ride. It's purpose is to transform passengers into builders, creators and implementers of an agenda.

If there are those among us who do not represent an agenda, or who reject or work towards the further suppression of our progress, we must give them distance and allow those political cowards to run for the hills and leave without them. Our movements for progress do not have room to carry more than we can handle. So please throw off other people's causes and baggage because we only have room for our own.

The *Nia Force* is the name of our liberating idea. It is how we transform dead brains into architects of an agenda. *Nia* is Swahili for purpose. In life we complete all successful undertakings with a purpose, or a goal. To make any goal successful or to give a goal reality, it must have action, or it is merely a dream. The *Nia force* is simply a purpose with action. A person who has a purpose with action is like a train in motion, as unstoppable as the flow of the Nile river.

The most important *Survival strategy* that one learns from the *Underground Railroad* experience is that in her efforts Harriet Tubman *never let the left hand know what the right hand was doing.* She never explicitly told anyone of her exact plans to escape or rescue *slaves*, not even the countless *slaves* who followed her. She mastered the art of deception to further her mission thus she too was unstoppable. Harriet Tubman once dressed like a man in a rescue mission to disguise herself from her captors.

Although slavery was an extremely vulnerable and hopeless position to be in, Harriet Tubman found empowerment from her spirit and her mind. She never believed that she was not free.

If we learn any lesson from the experience of Harriet Tubman, it is that before she was capable of helping others, she helped herself, and her family. We can not set out to save the world and work miracles in the lives of other people when our own families are in peril.

The *Underground Railroad* is a liberating concept that will lead you to change your approach to achieving your goals in life if you are able to select the correct path and remain on board to withstand even the most turbulent journey.

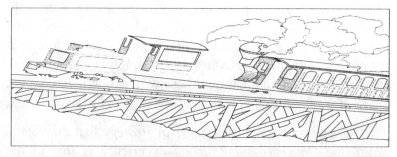

Get Black on Track!

9

RECONSTRUCTING BLACK CIVILIZATION!

"They stole it you must return it!"

There are a number of ways to make the Black community a better place to live. Here are just a few suggestions.

Stop *Black Bashing.* Stop is engaging in negative talk and destructive acts against Black people.
Look for the positive when dealing with the issue of "Black" or leave it alone.

Black should never be used as the explanation for why people commit crimes or abuse against Black people. People decide to commit baleful acts against Black people because they are sick. It is never because one is **Black.**

Develop an image code. It is critical that we develop an image code. The fashions of Black youth are derived from the prisons, gangs, etc. These same negative images are on television -- in videos, magazine ads and commercials.

Examine your own style of dress. How do you look when you leave the house? Make that essential change if necessary and set an example. Look around you what do you see? Do not be critical of others. The best way to achieve a positive result is to use positive influence by gaining the respect and esteem of others. A wise person once said, "*You do not condemn a dirty glass, you set a clean one right beside it.*"

R epair the temples. We have yet another task to perform and that is improving our health. The "slave diet" must be abandoned! Explore the possibility of changing your diet. It is interesting that many doctors are telling patients to alter their eating habits after they have had major surgery. Patients are advised to cut out red meat and foods high in cholesterol. Wouldn't it be more intelligent to maintain proper diets to prevent disease or surgery?

H old community lectures and discussions. Create support groups and counseling for those among us who are substance abusers, over weight or unaware of proper dietary habits.

A ction plan. Execute that program that you have been discussing for the last decade or so. You must do it now! For example, a number of people complain about newspapers and how they negatively portray the Black community. Don't just complain do something about it.

D evelop our own mode of responsible communication and media within the Black community. Begin by forming a community newsletter that apprises the public of topics and information. Aim to expand the newsletter to become a competitive source of information for Black people. Do not just complain or boycott with empty cups. Build your own institutions and support them.

"When two brothers fight another man reaps their harvest."

L earn to get along with other brothers and sisters. Stop bickering and squabbling about what some rich and famous celebrity is not doing for the people. Ask yourself what are you doing for yourself? How is your development and progress? Whom have you inspired and shared meaningful information with lately? Most of all, stop criticizing. It has often been said he who criticizes helps. Are you willing to offer any? Stop name calling especially in front of others.

He who sits in the middle of the road, gets hit by traffic moving in both directions. - African Proverb

S olutions. Be able to offer solutions to the problems and not just add to the rhetoric about what is wrong.

C onstructive dialogue. It is evident by the agenda and priorities of many Black organizations that our communities are lacking constructive dialogue. We need discussions and policy proposals regarding issues that directly effect our communities. Holding seminars, weekly lectures and community meetings will help us offer solutions to our problems.

Community forums and lectures will also enable us to maintain focus on building and changing things that we have power to change.

79

Our community efforts and attention should not be focused on anything over which we have no control. It is difficult to maintain focus when there are many things that distract us. Many so called politically enlightened groups will habitually spread information about "the system" that makes us feel powerless and eternally lulled as victims.

There is over emphasis on the fact that we are on the bottom followed by continual rhetoric about a *struggle*. As a result, our community dialogue is confined to steady volleying of rhetoric about what is wrong. We are oppressed people and targets of racism. We must stop this! It is a fact we are the international victims of racism. According to Dr. Frances Cress Welsing, we must understand the game that is being played on us and ask ourselves what are we going to do about it? Then do it!

According to Dr. Jawanza Kunjufu "we must awaken the cooperative spirit in the community." We can build businesses that serve the needs of our community. We can take control of the economics in our community. Do not shop where you can't work! Stop running with pockets full of money to other communities to shop!

The creation of a nation begins in the homes of its people.

A Black agenda is a program that is developed to address the needs of Black people effectively. It is a blue print of solutions, goals and project alternatives that are doable for Black people. In short, a Black agenda is developed by Blacks for Blacks betterment.

80

This is crucial in that too often other cultures have defined what agendas work best for the Black community. This is tragic because when other cultures plan our future or scarcely include us into their plans we lose and are again taken off track.

POINTS TO REMEMBER

✑ Never sanction a solution to a community problem that does not come from your community first. For example, do not allow other cultures to develop a rites of passage program to help troubled Black youth, or develop an educational curriculum for Black children. Do not permit anyone to suggest a curriculum for Black children without first reading Dr. Jawanza Kunjufu's, *Countering the Conspiracy to Destroy Black Boys.*

✑ Never allow any one to tell you that your goal is to achieve racial equality or any other similar self esteem attacking nonsense. Develop your own definitions and stop allowing others to define you, your circumstances or your future.

✑ Begin your agenda by analyzing first what you can do to better your self. Always do your homework first. Every idea or plan must begin with research.

〰〰〰

Chapter 4
WATCH THE CLOSING DOORS!

(ST-5) *Don't look back unless you want to go that way!*

10

THE YEAR 2000: A WAKE UP CALL
TO GET READY

"By the time the fool has learned the game, the players have dispersed."   - Ashanti

"The opportunity that God sends does not wake up him who is asleep."   - Senegal

By the year 2000 it is predicted that society will become more technologically advanced. To engage in simple daily activities such as, banking, parking, grocery shopping, education, research, using toll booths etc. -- we will need computer knowledge.

This new computerized society is also known as the information age. America has evolved from an industrial society to a society that now places its economic emphasis on information. It took America 100 years to evolve from an agricultural system to an industrial system. Yet it only took two decades for America to evolve into an information based society. This indicates just how rapid change takes place.

What does the information age really mean? It means that *"know how"* will be the ticket to financial security, social status, and overall advancement in society. More importantly

83

it means that a lack of knowledge or blindness to the changes in society will be disastrous.

There is a rapid increase in information occupations, where more than 60% of workers work with information as programmers, teachers, clerks, secretaries, accountants, stock brokers, managers, insurance people, bureaucrats, lawyers, bankers, and technicians. In an information based society the creation, processing, and distribution of *information is* the job.

America is becoming restructured. The changes that are taking place makes life seem uncertain. We all know that change is inevitable, yet many of us do not welcome it when it comes. The question is often asked, is there any way to anticipate future trends? Well, we can use the approach of modern American corporations and monitor local events and behavior.

According to some trend researchers, there are five major cities which set the trends that the rest of America follows. New trends begin in the local communities of, Tampa, Hartford, San Diego, Seattle, and Denver. Trends are discovered by studying the local newspapers in these cities.

California set a trend with respect to propositions 13 and 187. Connecticut was the first state to elect a woman governor in her own right and then Washington. Florida started the rush in condominiums and time shares. Colorado passed laws limiting growth of population, highways, shopping centers and housing units.

Trends are also studied in the Black community. Researchers study major cities that have a heavy Black population. Cities such as New York, Detroit, Los Angeles,

Atlanta, Chicago, Miami, Philadelphia, St. Louis, Jackson, Birmingham and the District of Columbia.

Why are trends important? Because trends affect our lives. Trends tell us the direction that the country is moving in. Trends, like trains are easier to ride when they are already going in our direction. When you make a decision that is in line with a trend, the trend helps you by giving you an edge. Even if you to buck a trend, you still have an edge because you know it is there.

Trends may be helpful in deciding what jobs to seek, where to live, or where to retire. A trend may help you decide whether to join a union, run for public office, or put your children in public school. Basically, a trend helps you evaluate society's events.

What will future trends mean to Black people? Those who are not prepared to meet the challenges of the year 2000 will fall through the cracks. There will be no need for unproductive people. People who can not read will not find jobs. People who can not follow rules and order will be behind bars. There will be no need for *useless* people in the future.

Who are the *useless* people? People who can not provide a service to further the interest of society. According to Sydney Wilheim in his book *Who Needs the Negro*, Negroes were brought to this country to work. The need does not exist today. In fact, a large percentage of the unskilled and low skilled jobs are being exported out of the country. It is estimated that 1.5 million jobs will leave the US by the year 2000.* The typical workplace will be smaller and most

85

new jobs will be in small businesses. Wages will become less equally distributed and part-time work will increase.

Individuals with education, training and are highly competitive will find the future challenging and rewarding. What does this mean to the Black community? There will be many opportunities for those who are prepared. The Black community must prepare to meet the future challenges head on.

It is predicted that U.S. corporations will spend some $900 million by the year 2000 on ads and promotions that are culturally diverse to attract a large consumer base comprised of people of color, i.e. African Americans, Hispanics, Native Americans, and Asians. It is estimated that people of color spend collectively $600 billion dollars on everything from toothpaste to automobiles and shoes.

African American consumers buy 18% of the orange juice, 20% of the rice and scotch & whiskey, 26% of the Cadillacs, 31% of cosmetics, 35% of soft drinks, 38% of the cigarettes, 39% of the liquor & 40% of the records and movie tickets. Research indicates that African American consumers are loyal toward "brand name" items. African Americans buy disproportionately more Tide, Uncle Ben's Rice, Aunt Jemima, Cigarettes, Quaker Grits & Oatmeal, Kraft, Southern Comfort, Seagrams, Cognac & many others. *

As a collective Blacks spend $460 Billion dollars on consumer items. Black people can not consume their way into equality. Productiveness is the only way to gain respect as a people. Black people cannot continue to be a consumer base without producing the goods that that they need. Take

Japan for example, the Japanese have produced themselves into a position of respect in the global arena. They produce automobiles and consumer items that are in high demand. The Japanese are non-white and are considered primary contenders in the global economic arena.

By the year 2000 it is predicted that people of color will be 30% of the economy. Will blacks own the publishing institutions, newspapers, magazines, cable TV stations, that companies will be forced to deal with if they want to reach the new *Multi-Cultural* consumer base?

By the year 2000 the American education system will be revamped to accommodate a culturally diverse community now in the majority. Will Black folk promote their unique and particular way of looking at the world, an African centered idea? Or will they continue to be parrots of the European way of thinking?

Will Blacks write their own curriculums and build their own schools or will they once again rely on other cultures to tell their story and track their children into special education concentration camps?

Computer technology will be necessary for all types of business transactions and business enterprises. Will Blacks learn the latest technology, design the latest technology or will they be consumed and surpassed by it?

American health care will be an important issue and area of focus. As the American population increases the life expectancy of individuals will also increase. Society will evolve from health care to *self-care*. Will Blacks continue to be the group with the worst health care and lower life expectancy or will they rely on their own doctors and

87

scientists to come up with answers and cures to diseases? Will Blacks take responsibility for their poor health by practicing preventive medicine and healthy diets?

American politics will become more sophisticated. Many Americans are abandoning the notion of traditional party loyalty and are voting based upon issues. Will Blacks become more intelligent voters or will they continue to follow behind a party in a predictable fashion like lambs going to the slaughter? Will Blacks continue to be predictable followers behind misguided leadership who is susceptible to selling out community loyalty for a piece of silver? Or will Blacks become independent mature thinkers who follow their own minds?

The answers to these questions are key to progress and survival. It means if Black people do not begin thinking and planning on important issues, they will continue to secure a position firmly pinned on the bottom of society. Existence for the benefit of others is slavery!

THE WORK FORCE 2000

Currently, there is immense controversy surrounding the American education system and its ability to educate students for the *work force 2000*. The Hudson Institute an Indianapolis based research firm has conducted a study on the American educational system that indicates that most high school students are not being properly educated for the future.

In fact, most students could not correctly determine the change due from the purchase of a two-item restaurant meal. The work force will demand that its entrants possess a high degree of skill, education and training. Will Black

Americans be work force participants in the future? Yes! Highly educated and skilled Blacks will have little difficulty in the work force. There will be more jobs for qualified Black entrants.

Contrariwise, it is predicted that in the year 2000 Black men will have the most difficulty entering the work force because of their current lack of training and preparation. Black people must begin preparing today if we are going to compete in a global market as a community.

As a result of America's inability to prepare students for the future, the U.S. is having great difficulty maintaining a leading position in the world arena. For example, the U.S. ranked 11 in top banks in the world behind Japan who owns the top 10 banks. Japan is the leader in automobile manufacturing, television manufacturing as well as other household consumer items.

Amid the failing educational system in America there is discussion about changing the present school curriculum to one that is more accurate and inclusive of diverse cultures. *Cultural Diversity* will have a visible impact upon society as it becomes less white male oriented while people of color will represent the greatest increase in population in the year 2000. *Cultural Diversity* has only become an issue given that the increase of population of immigrants have been primarily from two non-white cultures, Asian and Hispanic. Given that Hispanics range from Black to red to white they are considered diverse. Further, Asians also run the gamut of the color spectrum and can be considered diverse. Yet Black immigrants have never been considered diverse. Because these two groups, Asian and Hispanic have not assimilated into the "melting pot" it has caused America to redefine itself as *Multi-cultural*. Blacks have been classified upon race in America and not cultural status.

WHAT CAN WE DO TO PREPARE OUR COMMUNITY FOR THE YEAR 2000, THE ADVANCED TECHNOLOGICAL SOCIETY AND OUR FUTURE STAKE IN IT?

"The battles of the future, whether physical or mental, will be fought on scientific lines, and the race that is able to provide the highest scientific development, is the race that will ultimately rule."   Marcus Garvey

We can begin by stimulating invention, innovation, and creativity in our community right now! We can send more students to traditional Black colleges and encourage the study of science, mathematics and technology. We can provide community learning programs and workshops in computers, mathematics and technology. Take advantage of college programs that are offered as home study programs or computer on-line courses.(See study group chapter) We can invest the 460 billion dollars that we possess collectively towards our future.

This requires that we begin doing research, producing goods, services and necessary technology so that the African community can be among the various communities competing in the global arena. We can no longer look at our plight as a national dilemma but an international one.

We must look at the potential that the Black community has on an international level and if necessary consider our potential as a global corporation. We must look at the world as a "Global Village." This is not impossible when one looks at either Mexico or Korea and the impact in that these countries have had in world economical arena.

Take a trip through your closets and drawers and see how many products are made in these countries or outside of America for that matter.

As people of color we will represent the group of people who will experience a great increase in population. We must design our own agenda today if we are to survive in the future. We are all required to be architects of a program that includes building institutions, independent schools, economical enterprises, cohesive families, spiritual bodies and strong relationships.

We must take this message as a warning to get it together before we lose. Every home should be equipped with a computer and reference books. We must invest in the latest computer technology and abandon our consistent practice of buying large radios, televisions and cellular phones. These oversized electronic toys only pacify our people and will not prepare us for the future. Computer software should replace the extensive CD and audio tape collections found in most households.

Why must we prepare for the future as if our survival depends upon it? Because it does. We can not progress when we lack the basic education and technology that gives us access to information and opportunities once discussed primarily in *White Only* country clubs. Further, we must begin to think futuristic as well as in the present. Failure to do so will leave us further behind in our contest.

Although most will agree that there must be significant changes in education to accommodate the culturally diverse population that now permeates American schools there remains an antagonism towards the serious

91

implementation of change. The mere mention of creating a curriculum of inclusion, Multi-culturalism, or Africentrism in the public school systems across America is looked upon as too controversial and a threat to the American core belief system.

It appears that America is not ready just yet to give up the notion that Christopher Columbus discovered America. We can not wait until others are ready to accept the truth. We must begin to prepare now for the vast opportunities that await us. Our primary preparation must begin in the area of history and culture. The school systems must be corrected to reflect teachings that are truthful and have less emphasis on European myths.

However, I feel that we should neither wait on the school boards and other bureaucracies to decide our fate. We should not be dependent upon or demand that other cultures teach us our culture and heritage. Self-help is one solution.

While it is important for us to understand African history and culture we need a balance of the Africentric and Eurocentric thought so that we might be prepared as a people to compete in the highly technological society that is predicted in the year 2000. I mention the need to understand who we are because if Black people had better relations, half of the battle of what plagues us would be won. What can lead to a better relationship is a better understanding of who we are. Being well grounded in our blackness.

Additionally, we must grab the clipboard and lead the quest for cultural understanding. We can not allow other groups to use the *Cultural Diversity* debate to define who we are and determine where we will stand in the world arena.

AFRICENTRICITY- THE AFRICAN GENIUS

"History is a clock that people use to tell their time of day. It is a compass they use to find themselves on the map of human geography. It tells them where they are and what they are."

- Dr. John Henrick Clarke

"We must tell our story and tell it for ourselves..."

- Camille Yarbrough

A people with no history have no future!

We must tell our own story with our unique viewpoint of truth and that is from an African spirit. According to Molefi Assante, Africentricity simply means African people are the center of analysis. They are the subjects rather than the objects of study. Tony Martin, former professor at Wesleyan College, states that *Africentrism* is currently popular term for an idea that is as old as African American scholarly writing. It asserts that African people must construe their own reality and see the world from their own perspective. Africans should have a perspective of the world based upon Africa not Europe.

Professor Martin adds that *Africentrism* rejects both the claims of racists and the efforts of friendly but paternalistic representatives of other races to speak for the African. *Africentricity* has been constructed along the lines of re-centering Africans as agents of history rather than as objects on the fringes of Europe. Simply put *Africentricity* requires that when attendance is taken in the world frontier of human reality Africa is present.

Without a perspective of the world, we have lost the battle for our minds and are virtually just standing still on the

93

front line waiting to die. If we continue to define the family for example, as a mother, father and two children we will see our extended family relationships as dysfunctional. This European definition of a family will lead to the destruction of our lineage.

Eurocentrism presupposes that there is truth in denying Blacks as African and having any civilized humanity. It presupposes that everything worth acknowledging in the universe is uniquely a white discovery. That is simply a lie. We can conceptualize reality in an African way and restore truth to our vision. Truth is a universal statement that transcends time and national boundaries and no one has a monopoly on it.

✋ PITSTOP FOR PERSONAL INVENTORY

It is time for another pause to see how the passengers on this journey are doing. We have covered some very rough roads and you might be a little rattled. Remember answer the following questions as honestly as possible.

♦ Have you read a book about Africa?

♦ Can you think of any important lessons from history that might be helpful today?

♦ What acts have you taken to free your mind?

♦ Do you have a computer?

♦ Are you ready for the Work force 2000?

11

WHY YOU MUST READ

NO MORE USELESS PEOPLE!

"If you do not want a Black person to know about something print it..."

"Once you learn to read you will forever be free..."

Frederick Douglass

The first painful and familiar quotation above is a reality for many Black folks. People who do not make time to read and access information will miss out on the most lucrative opportunities. Our mere survival depends upon what we know and when we find out about the information.

Our history and contributions to humanity are hidden in books. The solutions to our problems are hidden in books. The answers to who we are and what our potential is -- is hidden in books. What we do not know will continue to kill us or keep us down. Reading teaches one what others learn from experience. We ask what is happening because we do not know what is going on. Ignorance testifies against us time again and we lose. Reading gives one a better vocabulary. A good vocabulary can lead to better opportunities in life.

You can improve your condition and become self-empowered by simply taking the time out to read. Take the first step to improve your attitude about reading. Pace yourself.

Begin your journey by clipping articles from magazines and newspapers. Read the newspaper daily. Read one book a month and increase. Make phone calls and write letters for free information at least once a month. Set a goal to expand your knowledge in an area in which you are unfamiliar. Take a visit to a local library once a week.

Self education is strength. Although it is possible everyone is not a potential college graduate. There are numerous reasons why people chose not to go to college. However, these reasons are never an excuse for staying ignorant or uninformed. Libraries are free and so are books in many cases. Do you have a library card? If not get one! Most local libraries hold book sales and educational lectures and seminars free to the public.

Use every spare minute you have reading. Always carry a small pocket dictionary with you while you read. This will help you expand your vocabulary. When traveling spend time reading a book or an article. If you read one book a week by the end of the year you would have read fifty-two different subjects. Marcus Garvey observed that,

> *"The greatest men and women in the world burn the midnight lamp. That is to say, when their neighbors and household are in bed, they are reading, studying and thinking. When*

they rise in the morning they are always ahead of their neighbors and household."

Build a home library of different subjects. Clip and save articles on current trends and future predictions, world events, science, technology, business, health, culture, and religion.

Spend 30 minutes each night reading before you go to bed. Read a newspaper magazine article, or chapter of a book. (Remember to counterbalance your information with the media from your own community, i.e., the *Black press*)

Research a topic that interests you with reference books at home e.g., business, investments, real estate, taxes, African culture, religion, etc.

PERSONAL INVENTORY

1. *Have you read a book in the last three weeks?*

2. *Do you subscribe to 4 or more magazines/Newsletters/Newspapers?*

3. *Is most or all of your reading materials on the same subject matter?*

4. *Do you own a dictionary?*

5. *Do you read every section of the newspaper?*

6. *Have you been to a library in the last three weeks?*

How To Get Black On Track!

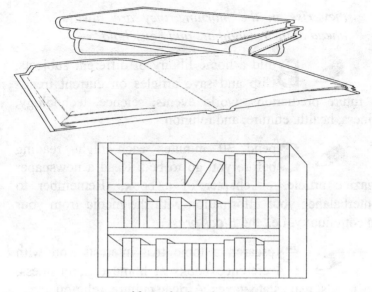

Knowledge is power!

If you answered *No* to 2 or more of these questions then you must read more.

HINT 1 - Locate a Black bookstore

HINT 2 - Join a book club or start your own

HINT 3 - Get a library card at the local library

HINT 4 - Get a magazine/newspaper subscription

HINT 5 - Read bulletin boards, flyers, newsletters, bumper stickers

HINT 6 - Increase your vocabulary by using new words in your daily conversation

12

DETOUR TO THE INFORMATION SUPER HIGHWAY
A LOOK AT CYBERSPACE

The political readjustment of the world means that those who are not sufficiently able, not sufficiently prepared, will be at the mercy of the organized classes for another one or two hundred years.
- Marcus Garvey

On this next stop we will visit the information superhighway to learn about the information age and computer technology. Information will be the greatest resource and industry for the future. Access and entrée into various arena's of society will be based upon "know how." The computer is a tool for gaining access to invaluable information.

The leaders in the information age use "know how" to tap into resources and experts without much effort. They are able to reach vital information first, well ahead of the masses. They are also able to process and manipulate data in a profitable way.

The information super highway, also known as *Cyber Space* is an interconnected network of computers hooked up by telephone, fiber optics and other high capacity lines. Each computer can communicate with others around the world. This network of computers is essentially an international community.

Are there any practical advantages of traveling down the information super highway? Absolutely! Imagine being able to know the stock quotes before a broker. Or the local news and world events before a news reporter. Suppose you were able to prepare your children with an elementary education before they entered the first grade. Imagine having access to information about the latest medical procedure, or cure before your doctor, or the latest legal opinions before your lawyer.

Just think, wouldn't it be great if you could perform home health tests before you entered a doctors office. What would an auto mechanic think if you knew what was wrong with your car before he/she even looked under the hood. What money, time and energy could be saved. Think about what an edge you would have on the rest of society. The information superhighway would enable you to access information before the so-called experts.

You could take the lead in business. Provide self-help solutions to many of the social problems that stem from a lack of education. The *Internet* would be a short cut route for Blacks to make up for 300 years in last place in the world arena. Black people could excel at the game with vital information.

Information is important for all of the essential aspects of life. We need information on the trends in the job market, housing, health care, business and politics, etc. Given that one of the major concerns in Black America is the inability to effectively communicate with each other the *Internet* would provide us with a forum to dialog internationally. We could compile global mailing lists of potential customers to market products and services.

All of this technology discussion sounds complicated, but it is really simple. What it really means is that Cyberspace can bring people closer together. *Cyberspace* can be used as a medium for Black people to talk to each other about solutions to social problems. With resource information on education, we could start home schools for children as well as adult continuing education programs. We could get the training in technology to become competitive for the work force 2000.

New jobs in service industries in the year 2000 will demand much higher skill levels than the jobs of today. Very few jobs will be created for those who can not read, follow directions, and use mathematics. There will be more joblessness among the least skilled and less among the most educationally advantaged.

Cyberspace can be used to spark the creative spirit in Black people. It can also be used to awaken the entrepreneurial spirit in the community. Why is it important to have an understanding of technology and *Cyberspace*? By the year 2000 it is predicted that most homes will have some type of terminal for accessing a digital telecommunications network. This network will connect most businesses and many homes with fiber optic links of great capacity. With this network, home shopping and banking, entertainment, or working from home will be a reality. Those who do not prepare will be left behind.

101

How To Get Black On Track!

What is the *Internet*? It is an"*internetwork*"-- a network of networks. Thousands of computer networks at businesses, universities, government agencies and libraries are connected by telephone, fiber optics and other high capacity lines.

A person can hook up to the *Internet* by building a connection with a computer system that is on the "Net" either through an on-line service, workplace, local *Internet* service provider, a bulletin board system, or maybe a library, school or government agency that offers free low cost connections.

Five million host computers are connected to the *Net*. The Internet is used by businesses, selling products, students doing research, brokers, hobbyists, political organizations and even kids. According to some the *Internet's World Wide Web* offers small Black businesses an inexpensive way to market goods and services to a vast audience of Blacks and others. An estimated 10 million to 30 million people world wide use the *Internet*.

World Wide Web

The Web is a site on the Internet that is a resource. Information on the Web is colorful and arranged in pages. The screen looks like a newsletter or magazine.

Bulletin Board Service

Bulletin boards are areas where people can post messages. These messages can be read by anyone who accesses the particular board. All messages posted to the groups central address are distributed to the mailboxes of subscribers, each have an opportunity to answer them.

E-Mail

    Electronic mail is transmitted by computer. A person can write a note and send it to another person via computer hooked up to a modem. E-mail allows people to communicate through On-line services, electronic postal delivery and fax. A person can send, reply or forward a message. It is a very fast way to communicate.

    The Internet is a common carrier of information. It is a shared link between people who use a variety of different services to access its resources. You can use E-mail to sign up for mailing lists, electronic discussion areas where people exchange messages on a whole library of topics ranging from Astronomy to African Spirituality to Jazz music.

Resources - On-line services

Prodigy - 1-800- 776-3449

CompuServe 1-800- 487-9191

America On-line 1-800 -827-6364

Delphi 1-800-695-4005

Books: The African American Resource Guide to the Internet, On Demand Press.

Tony Brown On-line.* Tele. (212) 575-0876   Fax (212) 391-4607.

Places To Visit

Melanet - http://www.ip.net/melanet/

Net Noir - http://www.netnoir.com/

AFRINET@CENTRAL PAGE -
http://www.afrinet.net/afrinet/central/center.html

AFRO-AMERICA NEWSPAPER SITE

http://www.afroam.org/

103

Chapter 5
DESTINATION NON-STOP TO EXCELLENCE!

(ST-6) *The train is going to go forward, there is no turning back. You have three choices, you can watch it pass, stand in its way, or get on board.*

13

HOME BASED STUDY GROUPS

The Learning Center - *The Sankofa Schule (School)*

*We will advance in the future only with the
knowledge of our past*

*Go back to fetch it symbol of learning from the past
in building the future   - Sankofa*

On this stop you will learn how to set up a study group. A study group is an excellent way to further the mission of spreading information, and building better relationships with other brothers and sisters.

A study group is also a very good back up plan for educating young people when the school system fails to teach the truth. We need to create forums to advance communication and constructive dialogue in our community.

How does one form a study group without people being turned off by the word "study"? What does a study group do?

A study group is a gathering of people to learn, discus topics, and share ideas.

1 ➤Select a small group of people who are open minded and have positive attitudes. 3- 5 people is a good number to begin. No more than 10! You do not want the group to become unmanageable. Remember stay on track!

This may seem difficult at first. It is not necessary to invite many people. You only need a few interested people. When the group becomes more cohesive, group members will invite friends, family and others. You will use half the energy required to organize a party to organize a study session.

2 ➤Choose a day of the week that is convenient for everyone to meet. Once you get started the group may meet at different times a week to accommodate the schedule of more members. I suggest Saturday or after business hours on Friday. You can begin by holding a meeting at your home.

3 ➤Take attendance at the beginning of every session. Make attendance mandatory and establish a policy for absence, and lateness.

4 ➤ Establish the requirements for membership at the first meeting of interested persons. Draft a charter for rules of conduct and procedures for group members.

5 ➤Choose the roles of each member and responsibilities. There should be a *Historian,* a *Scribe* or *Record keeper*, a *Librarian* who maintains the clip and save file, and a *Treasurer* to collect dues. The group can elect a *Moderator*. The *Moderator* must direct and facilitate the group sessions. Remember maintain order.

- ✍ Establish group rules and regulations at the first meeting. Do not allow visitors or tape recording of any kind to the study group sessions. Do not allow picture taking.

- ✍ Take attendance at the first session and exchange phone numbers at the end to establish a buddy -- buddy system. Make a schedule for carpooling our provide bus schedules for group members.

- ✍ Establish goals for the study group and devise a charter for the group that all members work on.

- ✍ Handout a written syllabus that outlines the topic that will be presented and important points to focus on. Make certain that you include a brief break or intermission in the middle of the session on the syllabus.

- ✍ The room that the study session is held should look serious. Arrange the furniture and chairs in an orderly fashion. I suggest a circle so that you maintain the learning environment yet it is communal.

Your study group may turn into a jam session although you had good intentions. It does not take much to tempt a group of people who still subconsciously expect that type of social event to occur every time two or more are together. Further, it is imperative that we be of sober mind and body when learning. No alcohol or smoking!

Study group Rules and Regulations

1. No visitors permitted (Advance approval by group members only)

2. All members must come on time to meetings

3. Members must call if late or absent

4. No talking out of turn

5. Respect will be given to all ideas and members

6. No talking during presentations

7. No music or loud noise during the meeting

8. No alcohol or tobacco permitted during the meeting

9. No picture taking or recording of meetings (Advance approval by group members only)

10. No Black bashing, gossiping or criticizing

11. Members agree to participate in discussions and projects

12. Members agree to honor the study group purpose statement

13. Members agree to read, study and research

14. New members will be permitted every 4 months

✐ The First Study Session

Begin the first study group session by choosing a topic. Then choose an activity such as video night or audio speeches to attract interest. Ask group members for suggestions. (See listings of video clubs and businesses.) The video or presentation should not exceed 2 hours in one setting. If the presentation is longer than 2 hours, break it up into two sessions for the following week. You want to permit the group enough time at the end to engage in a discussion. Material is easier to digest when broken down into parts.

* Serve only wholesome foods and drinks. Do not make the mistake of playing loud music and serving wine or alcohol.

* At the end of each session plan a round table discussion of the issues focused on.

* Remember to be patient and always allow everyone to speak. We will not all see things the same way at the same time when we have discussions. Emotions will flare because people have strong viewpoints. Be respectful and do not try to preach or permit other group members to do so. The purpose of a study group is to teach. Remember, *each one teaches one!*

* Make certain to focus your energy only on constructive dialogue and do not reduce the meeting to gossiping and squabbling sessions. Be careful to organize the discussions so that this does not happen. You may have to rigidly structure all the discussion and activity for the first 4 meetings.

The *Blue Nile* Study Group Outline

PURPOSE STATEMENT: To research and study African history and culture. Restore consciousness and truth to the African experience. Provide an open learning environment for people of similar values. Discuss history in the context of devising solutions and strategies to excel as individuals and as a community.

6:00 PM - Welcome - Refreshments (Healthy beverages). Allow members to pick up information from the information table. (Control Center)

6:10 PM - *Moderator* - Greetings - Remarks or the business of the day.

6:20 PM - Libation, meditation, recitation of the group purpose statement. (Form a circle)

6:30 PM Introduction- Topic *The Nile Valley Civilization.* Video Presentation. 1 - hour

7:30 PM Break - Refreshments

7:45 PM   Group discussion

8:15 PM   Closing remarks - (Donations) Libation and Affirmations. (Form a circle)

The *Scribe* takes minutes on the meeting and at committee meetings. The *Historian* prepares a brief summary of the presentation. Group members can alternate each week as the group *Historian.* The *Librarian* organizes information for the information table and future sessions. The *Treasurer* collects dues or donations from group members and keeps an accounting of all funds and transactions.

Video presentation of Anthony T. Browder, **Ancient Egypt: New Perspectives of an African Civilization.** (2-hours) 2 sessions

✓ Points To Remember

* 1   *Keep your study group private*

* 2   *Set goals & outline group rules and regulations*

* 3   *Stay on track (stay focused) always have a topic*

* 4   *Stay organized*

* 5   *Celebrate your progress*

* 6   *Practice the Nguzo Saba (Libation, affirmation)*

Note: Do not slant the study group sessions to any particular religious ideology. Group members will have different economic, and religious backgrounds. Focus on culture instead. The goal should be unity without uniformity.

Activity: Devise a name for your study group that is African. This should be the groups' first project. Group members should define the name and historical origins. Use an African book of names to research the name for the study group.

Design a logo for your group. Display your logo, name, and purpose statement prominently for all meetings.

111

THE UJAMMA STUDY GROUP *ૐ*

Ujamma *is a Swahili word that means cooperative economics.*

Purpose Statement: To research and study African history and culture. Restore consciousness and truth to the African experience. Provide an open learning environment for people of similar values. Discuss history in the context of devising economic solutions and strategies to excel as individuals and as a community.

6:00 PM - Welcome - Refreshments (Healthy beverages). Allow members to pick up information from the information table. (Control Center)

6:10 PM - *Moderator* - Greetings - Remarks or the business of the day.

6:20 PM - Libation, meditation, recitation of the group purpose statement. (Form a circle)

6:30 PM - Introduction- Topic *"Starting an Investment Club."* Group discussion and review of "The Investors Manual." From the *National Association of Investment Clubs.*

7:30 PM - Break - Refreshments

7:45 PM   GROUP DISCUSSION

8:15 PM - **Announcement**: Next Meeting (Hand out for *Control Center*) Read! Article: Black Enterprise Oct. 1990, "The Family That Saves Together," By Donna Whittingham-Barnes.

8:25 PM - Closing remarks - (Donations) Libation and Affirmations. (Form a circle)

Note: If the group decides to get a bank account I suggest that you follow the local requirements for registering a group or organization in your town. Contact your local government office, county clerk, or SBA, to find out the requirements.

A STUDY GROUP ROUTINE

Ask each member to clip an article from various periodicals either a magazine, newsletter, or newspaper, etc. Members should photo copy information for *the Control Center*. Every session should have a table where information can be placed for members to browse and share. Encourage members to bring information each session.

▓ THE CONTROL CENTER

The *Control Center* is a table where members can pick up or leave information for group members. This is where flyers and news clippings and newsletters, etc., should be placed. It is a community information center. The information table is called the *Control Center* because information is key to gaining control over our lives. Encourage members to bring literature to each session and photo copy it for the table. Use African fabric to decorate your *Control Center* and make it as visible as possible for all members.

CREATE YOUR OWN JOURNAL *"THE SCROLL"*

Each member should have a notebook to take notes and maintain their information. A notebook will help you organize information from lectures, seminars, and meetings. Part of your responsibility as a student is to study and easily access information for review. Make up a notebook for your mission. A loose-leaf notebook with folders is the best type.

ℰ-Create a section and label it for each type of learning activity that you attend.

ℰ-The first page should always include your aim or vision and a positive affirmation or inspirational message that will reinforce your aim.

ℰ-You can decorate the cover of your notebook with any images that reinforce cultural and political identity or agenda. Use symbols and expressions that are representative of who you are.

ℰ-Always leave a section for solutions and remedies. Label it "ACTION PLAN." This will help you to focus on a course of action.

THE PURPOSE OF THE NOTEBOOK -- SCROLL

The scroll is to be used as a reference tool. A *Scribe* is one who writes for the benefit of preserving data. Personal growth and development can be monitored by documentation. It is important that you write down ideas, solutions, and problems so that you can reinforce your agenda.

THE MEETING (NDABA THE FORUM)

This place is where you gather. It should have few interruptions. If you do not have a room at home, inquire about using a room at your local religious institution, community center or library.

Structure of the meeting when a speaker is present

❶ - The Control Center should always be at the entrance of the meeting room. Members should have easy access to information.

❷ - Serve non-alcoholic drinks and refreshments.

❸ - The speaker announces the topic and areas of discussion for the day.

The meeting should always include your "AGENDA" and evening topics. It is good to have a brief outline of the agenda (1 page) on the information table or handed out at the beginning of the lecture. This will ensure that the lecture is guided. Members can know what to expect for the topic of discussion. They can maintain focus on key points. If the activity is a video, audio, live lecture, or group discussion the speaker should make a few points before engaging in the activity.

❹ - Leave time for questions, and information sharing at the end of the program. Ask each member to comment about the issue. (Be respectful of different point of views)

❺ - Take a brief intermission so members can relax and ingest information but resume the agenda promptly.

NOTE: The computer is a valuable resource tool. The group can record information and store it on disk. If your group can acquire a computer it would be an excellent move. There are numerous on-line computer services that your group can subscribe to such as the *Internet, America On-line, Prodigy, Genie, CompuServe, Tony Brown Online.* The information highway is necessary to gain access to invaluable resources.

115

Here are some activities for a study group:

Project # 1 -- Write a purpose statement for the group/ individual members.

Encourage members to write *personal affirmations* or purpose statements. A purpose statement is what you aim to do and how you aim to do it. Remember, always develop an action plan.

Write a *group affirmation or purpose statement.* All members should participate. Hold think tank discussions of what the groups' mission should be so that individuals stay on track. Only allow positive comments and suggestions. Group members should also be inspired to present their individual affirmation or *purpose statement* to the group. Some members may be hesitant or shy -- do not force them to make oral presentations. Only those members who feel comfortable in sharing their *personal statements* should make oral presentations.

At the beginning of each meeting and/or at the end one person should recite the *group affirmation.* At the end of the meeting the group should form a circle and use the powerful energy of the circle to reaffirm their individual affirmations, or recite a phrase that will remind them of what they need to do. Leave each meeting focused to achieve part of the affirmation. At the end of the study group session go home and immediately work on your goal. Examples of *Purpose Statements*:

♦ **1-** Complete my education and strive toward self awareness, cultural and spiritual development. Build my community by creating competitive institutions.

◆ **2-** Become gainfully employed so that I will be able to support my family.

◆ **3-** *A GROUP AFFIRMATION:* S*tudy our story and learn the truth about the African experience.*

◆ Write the group affirmation or purpose statement and make copies for all members to keep in their notebooks.

Project # 2 -- Institution Building -- A reference library or information access library

1. Clip and Save File. Encourage the group members to start a clip and save file of various topics, current events, or history. Information can be gathered from newspapers, magazines, newsletters, periodicals, or on-line services.

Clip and Save articles from various periodicals and put them into a folder to be filed. The folder should be stored in a file -- a cardboard box will do. Each member should make a photo copy of information so that they can store it in their own home library and their notebook. (See section on the Scroll.) Develop your own filing system by date or subject that ever works best for you.

NOTE! Begin the study group sessions by always focusing on a topic, e.g., *Miseducation, Nile Valley, Ancient Kemet, Yoruba, Ahkan, Racism, etc.*

NEVER end the study session in an argument. If there is an issue that is controversial or contentious, simply ask all members to go home and research it and return the next meeting with intellectual debate.

NEVER end the study session with loud music or other distracting activities. Always END on a positive note, with

117

an open ended question so that members look forward to research and discussion the next week.

Project # 3 -- Develop a group reference library

Encourage group members to buy books and information. (See resources.) Bring books to all meetings.

Keep books and articles in the study room so that members can reference questions on hand. (See the list of reference books and materials at the end of this book. Buy new and used books. Go to the local library -- tag sales, etc.)

Project # 4 -- Group trips

Attend lectures by Black scholars to add insight and reinforcement to the groups learning. Set a goal to spread and share as much information by the year (2000...) Go to libraries, museums, rallies, plays, historical sites.(see resources at the end of the book).

Project # 5 -- Book discussion

Choose a book for the members to read. Discuss one chapter at a time so that the session is orderly and everyone can keep up with the reading. Too often it is overwhelming to discuss an entire book in depth in just one setting. Invite an author, or scholar to lecture to the group.

Project # 6 -- Book Review

Write a book review after the group has read and discussed a book. Publish the book review every 4 months in a pamphlet and distribute them to the community. Market the pamphlets to friends and other community members.

Project # 7 -- Write a group Newsletter

Compile information in a newsletter. All members should contribute to putting it together. Some members may write or edit articles. Other members may do the artwork and distribute the newsletter to local groups, schools, or churches. Remember be positive and do not publish gossip or Black bashing stories. You may organize the group to sell advertisements. Solicit advertisements from local businesses.

Project # 8 -- Educational Video Lecture

If a group member has a video camera borrow it or rent one from a video store. Make a video of your educational lectures. Market and sell the video. All members should participate in some aspect of the video production and distribution. Show the finished product at a study group session.

Project #9 -- T-shirts

Design a T-shirt with a cultural, spiritual, economic, or political message. Sell the T-shirts to group members, family and friends. Encourage group members to wear the T-shirt to study group sessions and events.

Project #10 -- Kwanzaa

Organize a Kwanzaa celebration for the study group. Allow each member to actively participate in the celebration. (See resource section at the end of the book for information).

Project #11-- Organize a Community Event

Rally, Expo, Lecture, Kwanzaa, etc. Form a committee to plan the event. Consult a book on event planning. This is the perfect fund-raiser for the study group.

Project # 12 -- Community Service

Start a clothing or food drive for needy people. Get study group members to collect an item to donate to a local shelter or community organization. Collect canned goods, winter coats, books, etc.

Project # 13 -- Resource Guide

Publish a Black resource guide in your community. Compile a listing of local Black businesses, services, and organizations. Solicit advertising from businesses. Market and distribute the directory to the community.

Project #14 -- Research Project

Choose a topic or issue and have group members do presentations. Take a trip to the local library or Black history library to conduct your research.

NOTE: With all the ideas on publishing keep in mind that you will want to copyright protect all material. Write the U.S. Copyright office in Washington DC for information.

✔ Which path to begin 10 Tips:

1- Establish group rules and formalities

2- Make it mandatory that all members will have an opportunity to speak and ask questions.

3- Do not embrace any particular religious ideology. (Group members may be from all different religions, economic or cultural backgrounds, e.g. *Jamaican, Haitian, Brazilian*).

4- The members of the group should dress comfortably or as culturally expressive as possible.

5- Make certain that the room where sessions are held is conducive for learning.

6- Put up positive images of Black people as visual aids. Keep your African art collection in the room. Burn incense, (Jasmine, Sandalwood, etc.)

7- Serve herbal tea, ice water, decaffeinated coffee, natural juice. Do not allow smoking!

8- Each group session should have a theme and mission statement.

I attended The Cress-Welsing Institute lectures in Washington D. C. The main topic of discussion was Countering Racism 2000. It is important to have a theme so that we positively move toward the goal of working toward a solution to our problems. It is okay to analyze and identify a problem and discus it however, the "Task Master" develops a solution and implements it. A theme will make the group stay more focused.

9- Become an emissary and share information. That is, spread your knowledge and information to others.

10- Commit yourself to reading books for and about African people.

SUMMARY

- Subscribe to a publication (see listings on publications and newsletters)

- **BUY BLACK!** Support Black institutions. Take the group to a Black owned business and make purchases.

- Unity Dinner! Hold an ethnic buffet of foods from the African Diaspora.

- Form a support group for members who have problems and need sisterhood or brotherhood.

START YOUR OWN HEALTHY EATERS GROUP

You have decided your eating habits must change. You now need the support and influence from others who feel the same way about their diet. Work toward your healthy eating goal with others by forming a group. Select a group of potential members from your community organization, family and friends.

☞ Plan your first meeting carefully. Choose a place where you will have the fewest distractions. Organize your meeting just like a study group session. *(See previous section on study groups).*

☞ Ask group members to clip and save articles and information on health and diet to be used in group discussions. There are a number of books that are helpful in getting you started. *(See resource section at the end of the book)*

☞ Discuss and identify the health problems of the Black community. Adopt an organization to help you. You may not have the power to change the eating habits of the entire Black community overnight but you do have the power to influence those who are in contact with you.

☞ Contact health and medical organizations for information. *(See resource section at the end of the book)*

☞ Discuss solutions to dealing with health problems. Group members may wish to share personal experiences. Remember, be patient and follow the same rules for group conduct in the study group session.

ACTION IDEAS

☞ Clip and save coupons and discount information to be shared by members. Make this information available at the information table.

☞ Members should bring wholesome recipes for the information table.

☞ Organize an event where each member brings a wholesome food, drink, or snack to the meeting. If members can meet at least once a month to introduce new food ideas and enjoy a relaxing meal, this reinforces and encourages changed eating habits.

☞ Hold a cooking session at a group members' home.

☞ Locate a local Black owned business in your community who serves wholesome food and patronize it. If one does not exist, it is a good opportunity to create one.

123

Network and discus business. Hold meetings, dinners and activities at a local restaurant.

☞ Publish a cookbook with the recipes from the Clip and Save file.

☞ Video tape cooking sessions so that the group can market and sell.

☞ Information file -- Can be used as a reference center to publishing a newsletter, book, pamphlets to distribute throughout the Black community.

☞ Develop a health product that is marketable

☞ Hold happy hour and only serve natural juice or punch. Do not serve soda, alcohol, or wine.

Before sharing in the feast always remember the ancestors. A libation or blessing affirms the goal to achieve a better diet in the Black community. Changing eating habits is very hard. Some members will be a little resistant.

Have patience and know this is a result of over 400 years of poor eating patterns that are not going to go away at one meeting. It requires spiritual support, discipline and determination. Many Blacks devour alcohol and tobacco regularly, so their goal might be to cut down at first.

☛ *Embrace the idea of eating healthy and make it your goal to encourage another person to change his/her eating habits. Set an example at holiday celebrations and family dinners by eating healthy and breaking the cycle of the slave diet.* **AIM:** *Change and improve the eating habits of the Black community by changing or improving your eating habits.*

Recommended Reading

Heal Thyself, Quen Afua, A&B Books Publishers

African Holistic Health, Llaila O. Afrika, A&B Books Publishers

Tissue Cleansing Through Bowel Management, Bernard Jensen

Eat To Live, Ellijah Muhammad

Heal Thyself Cookbook, Diane Ciccone, A&B Books Publishers

Joy of Juicing, G&S Null

Spiritual Nutrition Handbook, Keith Wright

Juiceman's Power of Juicing, Jay Kordich

Dick Gregory's Natural Diet for Folks Who Eat: Cookin' with Mother Nature. New York: Perennial Library.

"When your hand is in the lions mouth, be careful how you take it out."   -Liberian Proverb

"The way water moves on the surface is not the way it moves on the bottom."   - Liberian Proverb

"Not through height does one see the moon."
- Nigerian Proverb

"De noise of de wheels don't measure de load in de wagon." -African American Proverb

14

NETWORKING

"A single bracelet does not jingle..." - Congo Proverb

A sophisticated meaning of "Networking" is an interconnected organization or system. *Networking* is also defined as a chain of interconnected people trading information. For our purposes "Networking" will be considered as the bringing together of Black people to exchange information, advice and moral support.

A *Network* can be a valuable asset for survival in business as well as life. It can provide one with information about almost anything. It can be a route to attaining goals of independence, control and often power if used correctly. The most important thing to remember in Networking is that a *Network* is only as good as the information and people it contains. Connecting with the right people is sometimes a difficult task, however it is not impossible. One can attain the ultimate and effective use out of a network if it is put together with the following factors in mind:

✔ *Do not beg for anything*

✔ *You can not get something for nothing*

✔ *You must always return something for taking something*

✔ *Have patience*

✔ *Never take more than you give*

A successful network does not happen over night. Outright begging for information, employment, a service is the fastest way to make people lose confidence in you. It will close down options for an even exchange of information.

Make a list of people, businesses, or services you already know. Collect business cards. Next make a list of those things you are interested in doing. Express an interest in your contacts. Let them know what exactly you are interested in doing. Keep a network directory using file cards or a business card holder.

At the outset your list may be small and seem meaningless. It is the foundation of what will be an enormous resource. It is important you begin to build your list with persons who have a positive attitude and who will exchange information and not always take. They must also provide moral support, be competent and stimulating.

Enhance your network socially. Like anything else growth is cultivated. It is always good to go to social functions where people with your interests can provide you with resources, information and new contacts.

Do your homework! First evaluate yourself and determine your values and goals. Before results can be realized, before you buy index cards and a file box, before you collect a single business card, define your values.

Values, goals and aspirations will effect the outcome of your resource bank. If you build your resource bank with a bad foundation, faulty values and selfish goals, the resource file will stand lob sided. It will stand with the threat of collapse each time you add a new contact.

Purchase either a file box with index cards or an address book. Include the names -- addresses and telephone numbers of people whom you already know. Include businesses, services, and educational resources in your file. Include names of individuals who can provide more names of other valuable people or services. For example:

"...*Who can be of service*

(a) *a resource person*

(b) *Conduct a service*, i.e., an accountant, attorney, typist, guidance counselor, librarian, plumber. Organize cards and information by category. You now have a resource bank.

Networking is an individual process. It begins by you carefully following the guidelines that you set up at the beginning of your venture and following them through to the end. Information is the link that binds people to people. A *Network* knows no limitations. The individual is very important in Networking. A person may either be a link to other information or on the receiving end of information. A *network* will enable you to change those elements in society at first glance appear to be obstacles. Make a list of the things that you are interested in or need. Education is very important. One must seek advice or counseling from contacts.

129

The process of *Networking* must include our elders, because they are important resource tools for our community growth. They have knowledge and experience that we can draw upon to enable us to focus on where we need to make progress or modify tactics. When we generate more discussions with our elders that is, create forums, conferences and think tanks -- we can gain useful strategies. The forums and meetings will allow us to network with other organizations. *Networking* with each other is key to obtaining maximum community participation and results.

We must fully use our own channels of communications within our own Black organizations, fraternities, sororities, religious and spiritual, cultural, and political organizations. If you can choose the most progressive minds of each organization you can expand your circle of influence and promote power and change among the greatest number of people. If you isolate yourself from groups you will be by yourself and fail in your effort to achieve your goals.

We may often disagree with the objectives of many of our Black organizations. It is easy to criticize organizations that we do not belong to. It is also counterproductive to focus our energy on what certain Black organizations are not doing for the community. This negative attitude must be replaced with positive action solution thinking. Instead of condemning an organization ask yourself the critical question, *what are you doing for the community?*

Seek out organizations that can work toward a positive end. Remember, an organization is only as good as its members. If you are a member of an organization or association, set a goal to become active if you have been an inactive member. Use your contacts to bring about change and positive programs in your community.

B egin networking with members in other organizations. *Networking* is the most effective way to get people who otherwise would not get along in one group to work together towards a common goal. The memberships in most of our organizations are loyal and consistent. They have a group identity that is hard to challenge.

It is unrealistic right now to think that all organization members will leave their respective group to form one big association of Black people and give up their individual group identity. The idea of networking is basic to grasp how different organizations can achieve a unified end.

Networking allows each person or organization to keep its own identity while being called upon to sponsor and support a community venture. Any group or organization that does not wish to come together to promote learning, literacy or other solutions should be avoided until they are ready. (See section NDABA) All of our institutions should embrace this idea. If we do not have institutions that are cooperative we must build new ones and leave the old ones behind. A good community event that requires a cooperative effort is Kwanzaa or a cultural festival that includes lectures by elders. Read - *Success Runs In Our Race, George Frasier.*

IDEA: Hold a community *Teach-In.*

CONCLUSION

Moving From Theory To Practice

"When the snake is in the house, one need not discuss the matter at length..."   --Ewe Proverb

All the information and education that we receive sometimes make us eager to share it with everyone. We become self appointed emissaries trying to spread and share our newly acquired intelligence. We get excited and motivated to diagnose everyone around us. We quickly and forcefully impose therapy programs on our friends and families. We want to limit ourselves to dealing only with *Africentric* or like minded people.

At some point we discover that it is much easier to deal with people who share the same ideas as we do. We will scoff at or engage in heated debates with non-believers or those who are still resistant to our teaching. We become impatient and overly sensitive to criticism from others about our lack of interest in partaking in activities that we once enjoyed before we became "conscious." We have quickly discovered that our circle of associates and friends has become very small and so has our circle of influence.

Before we disassociate ourselves from too many people or become too judgmental and hypercritical let us first do some self analysis. It is key we understand what has taken place. All of the reading, lectures and research we have acquired has made us grow.

Keep in mind that growth is an individual thing. We can ask a thousand people what is the state of Black America and get a thousand different answers. The answers to that question is all relative to ones experience and can only be answered individually. Begin by asking yourself "what state are you and your family in? If everyone concentrated his or her efforts on self improvement the 'state' of Black America would improve overnight. This is not to say all things and conditions will change because we change.

Again only those things we have power to change should be our main focus. We have the power to change our attitudes, our eating habits, our level of education and self awareness our ability to take care of ourselves. Most of all we have the power to change our spirit. There are cases where we can not and should not try to plant seeds on a dessert. This is not to say we should condemn the lack of understanding and awareness of some brothers and sisters. Instead just set the example of what self-realization and understanding has done for our life.

Never get stuck at the stage of being reactionary to every bit of information you receive. This is a typical response of many Black people because we are very emotional people. That is probably how we survived most of the trauma of slavery without seeking immediate vengeance against our oppressors. It is always all right to become emotional about a situation. However, we need to move out of the emotional state with action or a higher mind power.

Too often we get angry about the dynamic of racism and our mis-education and we do not advance to viable solutions to countering the effects. When our study groups are formed they can be think tanks or what ever we want them to be.

We have the answers and the power. This is the practice part of the idea of *Getting Black on Track*. It is the most difficult part of the program to master. Do not allow yourself to get caught up in making your teachings a hobby. For example, some conscious and Africentric minded people faithfully read every book they can about racism and oppression. They attend every Kwanzaa, every Black history month event on their community calendar yearly. They attend every lecture, wear and collect all the paraphernalia, yet they never heed the messages. These very conscious and well-read people fully understand the dilemma of Black people yet feel powerless and overwhelmed.

Moreover, they feel helpless as to what they can do to counter the situation. Many of their activities are escapism from dealing with the realties that they spend all or most of their time either learning or talking about. At this point it is time to put many of the theories into practice. This is what I call an *arena of control*. The control arena is where one has the most influence and power to effect real change. The first place where one can begin is always with self. Next is with family and immediate persons that one comes into contact.

EPILOGUE
Letter To My Readers

September 29, 1994

Dear Friends,

I feel compelled to be both an advocate and instructor for getting Black on Track. It has been my experience we teach others the lessons we must learn ourselves.

My entrance onto the platform in search of "self" led me to rediscover who I am and develop a program for success and positive thinking. At a low point in my life, I discovered motivational tapes and self-help books on positive thinking and goal setting. I successfully used the principles I learned from various motivational speakers. I am an avid supporter of positive mental programming for folks who wish to become successful in life.

What most of the motivational material I came across emphasized was a strong sense of confidence or self esteem. This is often called positive self-awareness. Motivational material teaches one how to get excited about achieving goals. I learned that motivation comes from within a person and not from outside sources.

Most of the self-help and motivational material on the market focused on self-esteem, yet little of it specifically addressed the self-esteem problems of Black people. I was curious how a group of people who are made to feel inferior to all other cultures in society could consume motivational

135

material and feel self confident? I wondered if motivational material worked magic in dissolving all self-doubt and every self-complex?

I consistently asked myself -- Is it possible for Black people to apply success strategies to their lives daily although they are victims of racism and discrimination? Could a positive mental attitude really block out reality so one can cope with whatever difficulty life brings? I came to the conclusion success talk means nothing if a person feels empty and unmotivated inside.

My analysis of the problem led me to the understanding that some Black people need advice on how to rid themselves of reinforced negative thoughts. Also, Black people need instruction on how to maintain lasting self confidence in a less than friendly society and learn the truth about who they are.

During my spirituous journey in search of success I discovered a persistent need for wholeness that would not go away. I found Africa and restored consciousness, pride and a frame of reference to my life.

I like many others believed I had no link to a cultural heritage other than the tradition of shackled limbs and fear. I felt a need to locate the missing link to my experience and return to my roots. My study of Africa in a study group setting with other truth seekers, and my visit to Africa in books filled my cultural void and brought me to my destination of wholeness.

My personal trip to get Black on Track has guided me to write this book. This is not a history book. It is a self-improvement book to promote goal setting, planning and achievement in Black people. My aim is to guide other curious or confused Black people onto the right track to reaching the long overdue destination of self empowerment through cultural awareness. The phrase *Black on Track is really a code to achieve success in life.*

This book will not tell you anything I have not experienced myself. In fact, many of the points I mention are things I must also learn. I too have repeated many errors and have strayed from my goals in life. I have been sidetracked and derailed numerous times. As a result, I grew incredibly determined as a passenger on winding toilsome rides to get Black on Track and learn from my setbacks. I now have an agenda, established goals, master action plans, and a system of organization I would like to share with you.

As you attempt to get *Black on Track* you too *may* experience the same type of unwieldy journey occasionally back sliding, running head on into obstacles, and glaring often at familiar sights. Do not allow this to discourage you. Allow me to be the first to testify that the law of averages will always be on your side as long as you keep on trying and never give up on empowering yourself. Yes, you can do anything you put your mind to because you have the power inside you.

Getting Black on Track is a journey rather than purely a destination because it is something that does not happen overnight. We must work on this process daily. The train is a symbolic vehicle in this imaginary journey in search of self. To find out our station and standing in life many of us must often endure a mental trip complete with webs and drudges. More important, we must always keep moving like a train.

137

When you develop the *science of mind power* you see how important mind power, the right mental attitude and the role of independent thinking play in your life. A positive mental attitude might mean the difference between success and failure in your undertakings. It is your belief system and your attitude that will determine how prosperous, or successful you will become in life.

It is through the art of visualization one creates mental images as blue prints of goals in life. This type of mind power allows us to first visualize our ideal scene, then work at making it a reality. Some people call this dreaming. Well, dare to dream about that which you desire most in life, then add action to make those dreams a reality.

If you can not see yourself happy, successful, gainfully employed, or in a happy relationship it is doubtful whether you could become any of these things and more. Our imaginations are our work stations for creating that which we want most out of life. It is in the mind where we first design plans for action in our lives. Lose control of your mind and the ability to visually plan and you will lose control over your life.

You will go much farther in life if you hold the belief you are free, capable and well deserving. Visualize your ideas and apply the necessary action required to achieve your goals. Besides, you will not go very far if you believe you are undeserving or held captive by some imaginary force. The mission of true self discovery will lead you to find your inner strength.

This book was written to further Carter G. Woodsons' efforts to re-educate Black People. Carter G.

Woodson, 1875-1950, was the father of Black history week, an author, educator and one of the most brilliant social scientists of all times. I deal with the issue of education in the chapter *Why You Must Read* -- and it is a running theme all over this book.

In addition, this book was written to further Harriet Tubmans' efforts to set Black people free. Harriet Tubman was the conductor of the *Underground Railroad* 1820? - 1913, an abolitionist, nurse and military aid. I focus briefly on one survival strategy Harriet Tubman used in the chapters the *Underground Railroad* and *Survival Tools*.

There is so much discussion and analysis about the plight of African people's world wide that I do not want to add to this debate. The word Black in the title of this book should not de-emphasize the focus of Africa as the point of restoration or be understood as a denial of African heritage. The word Black is used so people who do not yet identify with an African consciousness are not turned away from the valuable information this book contains.

This book is for Black people who aim to focus their energy in a productive way, form an agenda, and improve the quality of their lives. The essence of *Getting Black on Track* is that change requires effort, commitment and discipline. There is no easy plan or road map but the one that you devise for yourself. This book does not contain all the answers to life's problems. This book is just a *wake up call*, a *tug on the coat tail*, a *beat of the drum* to get ready to make a difference in your life by starting with yourself.

I do not focus heavily on the root causes of the imbalance caused the African because I feel other scholars have handled that topic more effectively. At the end of the book I include a brief reading list of recommended starter books for home study.

I do wish to focus on what we can do rather than what we can not do because this gives us a sense of power. With so many dynamics challenging your life, you must focus and never lose sight of your aim in life and stay positive.

I do not profess to be an expert on success only a long time student in getting *Black on Track*. If this book can help someone else, then it is worth writing. If by chance you see me at the platform, I am getting it together again. Yes! I'm *Getting Black on Track*. My spirit is unbroken! I am on a MISSION!

Don't let anybody turn your train around! Stay on track with the power of your mind. Stay on course with the power of your spirit!

PEACE & POWER!

Alice J. Crowe

Why Get Black On Track...

...As long as the Black Race bears the universal badge of inferiority forced upon it by scientists who have distorted or suppressed Black history, there will always be those of us to focus on truth to return the Black race to its former position of respect and reverence on the earth... *Legrand Clegg

AGENDA

*H*ow to Get Black on Track is a Black self-improvement guide. This book is the pathfinder for putting you in the right direction in life by engaging you in a revolution of self. It is hoped you will create your own agenda, system of organization for learning, goal setting and ultimately self-empowerment. The purpose of this book is to preserve the scholarly works of the most brilliant thinkers and motivate readers to begin home school programs.

Our homes can become learning centers, and think tanks to building institutions and organizations in the community. Suppose Black people were to set up learning centers in their homes and use available information and resources -- it would not matter whether the education system in America was teaching Black history. Black students would be able to bring Black history with them into the schools and anywhere else. Black history month would be society's opportunity to play catch up to gain the knowledge that Black people already have. Does this sound too idealistic? Well, think about it!

Suppose Black people would properly use think tanks, that is hold their revival meetings for solution gathering, they could form networks and create self reliant communities. They could solve their own social problems. The best and brightest of the community would have a choice between the corporate auction block and their own enterprise. Blacks would no longer have to sell themselves to the highest corporate bidder wasting energy, and ingenuity for the sole benefit of other cultures.

What is more important, Blacks could win the battle being waged for their minds if they change television time to learning time, and replace music videos with educational videos. As the victor in the mind war Blacks could begin a new thought process of *seriousness of purpose* and think from an economic point of view to gain the edge. Blacks must first make a conscious commitment to **BUY BLACK** whenever possible and support their institutions and use patience while these businesses are growing. Business owners must network with each other to perpetuate their longevity in the community.

*H**ow to Get Black on Track* is a road map for people who have lost faith and confidence in themselves. The aim of this book is to awaken and rekindle all dead and sleeping spirits to action. Many Black people have become complacent in life. Some have broken spirits, broken dreams and broken minds. It is easy for disappointment to end all desire to strive and achieve in life.

There is a common expression used in performing arts, "W*hen in trouble fade to Black.*" When there is trouble or difficulty on the stage during a theater performance, the first thing that happens is the director shouts, "Cut the lights!..." Everything fades to Black until the problem is under control. Since this tactic works for a director why not try it! Fade to Black and recapture that positive spirit when you experience chaos in your life.

H*ow to Get Black on Track* can be used to
cultivate our existing *Survival Tools* so that we
can find the solutions to our problems and
strengthen ourselves and our community. The
most important thing to remember when faced with an
undesirable situation in life is, if the problem is one that you
have the power to change you take action. If the problem is
one in which you have no control over, leave it alone. Do not
waste your energy.

The key to getting what you want in life is to take
action. Help will come from the least expected sources when
you are putting your efforts and energy in the right direction.
Don't just sit still.

Once you begin knitting the spirits will supply the yarn.

The universe will always provide us with answers to
our problems. *Spirituality* means faith in self as a divine and
worthy expression of the creator and faith in spirit as our
pilot in life. A firm belief in ourselves coupled with faith in a
higher power will enable us to say to the world, Yes we can!

ABOUT THE AUTHOR

Alice T. Crowe was born in the Bronx New York and had lived in Rockland County for 22 years. She graduated from Adelphi University and holds a Bachelors degree in Political Science. She also holds a law degree from Howard University School of Law. She is an adjunct professor at a local college in Rockland County in Suffern New York. She is CO-owner and operator of Zola Africentric Gallery in Nyack New York.

Resources, further reading, and study

Baruti Kafele, Goal Setting for Serious Minded Black Folks of All Ages.

Les Brown, Live Your Dreams

Think & Grow Rich A Black Choice, Dennis Kimbro, Napoleon Hill.

Tapping The Power Within, Iyanla Vanzant

In The Spirit, Susan Taylor, Amistad

Success Runs In Our Race, George Frasier

Why should white guys have all the fun? Reginald F.Lewis & Blair S. Walker.

The Seven Habits of Highly Effective People, Steven Covey

First Things First, Steven Covey

OPEN YOUR MINDS EYE

The Isis Papers The Keys to the Colors, Dr. Frances Cress -Welsing, Third World Press.

The United Independent Compensatory Code System Concept, Neely, Fuller.

From Ancient Africa to African-Americans Today Portland: Portland Public Schools 1983, Asa, Hilliard.

Nile Valley Contributions to Civilization, The Institute of Karmic Guidance, Inc., Anthony T. Browder.

From the Browder File, Anthony Browder

No Justice No Peace, From Emmet Til to Rodney King, Terrence, Morris.

Message to the Black Man, Ellijah Muhammad

The African Origin of Civilization, C.A. Diop

Notes For An African World Revolution: African at the Crossroads, Africa World Press, Trenton, NJ. John Henrik Clarke.

African Origins of the Major "Western Religions." ben-Jochannan, Yosef, Alkebulan Books.

Metu Neter Vol. I , Amen, Ra Un Nefer, Khamit Corp.

145

How To Get Black On Track!

Africa's Gift To America, J.A. Rogers

Man, God and Civilization, John H. Jackson

Marcus Garvey, Message to the People: The Course of African Philosophy, edited by Tony Martin. The Majority Press

Introduction to African Civilizations, John H. Jackson

Afrikan People and European Holidays: A Mental Genocide, Rev. Ishakamusa Barashango

Visions for Black Men, Dr. Na'im Akbar

Golden Age of the Moor, Dr. Ivan Van Sertima

Kupigana Ngumi, Root Symbols of The Ntchru & Ancient Kmt, Vol.1, Shaha Mfundishi Maasi & Mfundishi J.H. Hassan K. Salim

Black Man of the Nile, ben-Jochannan, Black Classic Press.

Philosophy & Opinions of Marcus Garvey, Edited by Amy Jacques Garvey

What They Never Told You In History Class, Indus

Khamit Kush, Luxorr Publications

MAGAZINES/ NEWSPAPERS

Health Quest, The Publication of Black Wellness, 200 Highpoint Drive, Suite 215, Chalfont, PA 18914.

Your Black Books Guide-United Brothers & Sisters Communication Systems, 912 West Pembroke Ave., Hampton Virginia 23669, 1(804) 723-2696.

N.I.P Magazine
354 Hearne Ave
Cincinnati Ohio 45229

VIDEOS/ Audio Tapes

Yosef ben Jochannan, Nile Valley Contribution To Culture, Black Classic Press

Jackson, John G., John H. Clarke *"Hubert Henry Harrison: The Black Socrates"*

Legacies, Inc.
Jacqueline L. Patten-Van Sertima
347 Felton Ave.
Highland Park, N J 08904

ORGANIZATIONS

The Third Eye
Sponsors Annual
Conferences
PO Box 226064
Dallas, TX 75222
(214)748-1736

Dr. Jill Pookrum's Civilized
Medicine Institute
Jewel Publications
60 East Ferry
Detroit, MI 48202
(313)874-2100

Herb Work
At **Cottonwood Hot Springs**
Spa
P.O. Box 247
Cottonwood, Alabama
36320-0247
(205)691-3931

Kemetic Institute
Lectures/ Study Groups
700 East Oakwood Blvd.
Chicago, IL 60653
(312)268-7500

National Black Wholistic
Society
(Retreats/Conferences)
P.O. Box 69241
St. Louis, MO 63169
(314)382-5196

Journal of African
Civlizations
Ivan Van Sertima (Editor)
African Studies Department

Beck Hall
Rutgers University
New Brunswick, New Jersey
08903
African Echoes
Lecturers
147 West End Ave.
Newark, NJ 07106
(201)373-3826

1st World Alliance Lectures
400 Convent Ave. #1
New York, NY 10031
(212)368-7353

Black Unity and Spiritual
Togetherness
(BUST) Study groups w/ a
spiritual & Economic
Direction
PO Box 1088
Opelousas, LA 70570
(318) 232-7672

Ausar-Aset Society
1107 Atlantic Ave.,
Brooklyn New York 11216

Institute for Independent
Education
1313 North Capital Street NE
Washington DC 20015
(202)745-0500

The Institute of Karmic
Guidance
P.O. Box 73025
Washington DC, 20056
(301) 853-2465

147

Additional Reading & Ideas

Mind Over Money, Dave Davies, Success Dynamics, Vermont.

How To Buy Mutual Funds The Smart Way, Stephen Littauer, Dearborn Financial Publishing, Ill.

No-Load Stocks, How To Buy Your First Share & Every Share Directly From the Company - With No Broker's Fee, Charles B. Carlson, McGraw-Hill, Inc.

Black Economics, Solutions for economic and community empowerment, Jawanza Kunjufu, African American Images, Ill.

Study group ideas:

Project #15 -- Start an investment club

Contact the *National Association of Investment Clubs*, 1515 East Eleven Mile Road, Royal Oak Michigan 48067 - (313) 543-0612. Write for a guide to sound investment principles. "The Investors Manual."

See also, Black Enterprise Oct. 1990, "The Family That Saves Together," By Donna Whittingham-Barnes.

Project #16 -- Start an after school tutoring program

Organize study sessions for students. (GED, SAT & other type of exams). Begin with students from group members families.

Selected Bibliography

Akbar, Naim, 1991. Visions For Black Men, Mind Productions &Assocs. Inc.

Assante, Molefi, 1988. Afrocentricity, Africa World Press.

Beason, Jake, 1989. Why We Lose, Col D'var Graphics.

Bennet, Lerone, Lessons in Black History,

Bernard, Jacqueline, 1967. Journey Toward Freedom, The Story of Sojourner Truth, Dell Publishing, N.Y.

Bradford, Sarah, 1961. Harriet Tubman, The Moses of Her People, Corinth Books, New York.

Bristol, Claude M., The Magic of Believing, Prentice Hall Press.

Garvey, Marcus, Message to the People: The Course of African Philosophy, edited by Tony Martin. The Majority Press.

Hilliard, Asa, Dr., and Listervelt Middleton, Free Your Mind Return to the Source: African Origins, Waset Educational Productions, East Point GA, 1988.

Kafele, Baruti, Goal Setting for serious minded Black folk of all ages. Baruti Publishing.

Karenga, Maulana, 1977. Kawaida Publications. Kwanzaa: Origin, Concepts, Practice.

Martin, Tony, The Jewish Onslaught, Majority Press.

McFarland, Rhoda, Coping Through Self-esteem, The Rosen Publishing Group, New York.

Naisbit, John, Megatrends, 1982. Warner Books. See also Content analysis and the study of sociopolitical change, by Morris Janowitz in Journal of Communication, vol. 26, no. 4, 1976.

Subira, George, 1988. Getting Black Folks to Sell, Very Serious Business Enterprises.

Vanzant, Iyanla, Tapping The Power Within, Kayode Publications.

Wilḩeim, Sydney, 1971. Who Needs the Negro. New York: Anchor Books.

Welsing, Frances Cress, 1991. Isis Papers, Third World Press, Chicago, Ill.

How To Get Black On Track!

Woodson, Carter G. 1969. The Miseducation of the Negro, Assoc. Publishers.

Articles

The Art of War, Zen Tzu Success Magazine, March 1994

Nothing Else Has Worked. Buy Black, Bernard W. Kinsey, New York Times, Sunday August 1, 1993 p.11.

Work Force 2000, Work and Workers for the 21st Century, William B Johnston and Arnold H. Packer, Hudson Institute.

Ryan, Nancy, "Marketing to Black Consumers," Chicago Tribune, June 9, 1991, section 7, p.6. Tony Brown's speech, May 20, 1990, Freedom Fund Dinner, Jackson, Tennessee.

PCs In The Home, Bob Laird, USA Today Section E, June 20, 1995.

Black Business on the Internet: A Market that was 'Invisible Until Now', by Stephen C. Miller, New York Times, September 4, 1995.

Index

MAIL ORDER FORM

How To Get Black On Track

A SELF-EMPOWERMENT GUIDE

$10.00 pb

EYE OF ATUM PRESS

P.O. Box 88

Nyack, N.Y. 10960

The perfect gift for a friend or loved one

Shipping:

Book rate: **$2.00** for the first book and .75 cents for each additional book.

Payment:

Check or Money order to *Eye of Atum Press*

Allow 4-6 weeks for delivery